BESSBOROUGH

Three Women. Three Decades.
Three Stories of Courage.

Deirdre Finnerty

HACHETTE
BOOKS
IRELAND

Copyright © 2022 Deirdre Finnerty

The right of Deirdre Finnerty to be identified as the author of
the work has been asserted by her in accordance with the
Copyright, Designs and Patents Act 1988.

First published in Ireland in 2022 by HACHETTE BOOKS IRELAND
First published in paperback in 2023

1

Cataloguing in Publication Data is available from the British Library.

ISBN 978 1 52934 039 6

Typeset in Garamond Premier Pro by Bookends Publishing Services, Dublin.
Printed and bound in Great Britain by Clays Ltd, Elcograf S.p.A.

Hachette Books Ireland policy is to use papers that are natural, renewable and
recyclable products and made from wood grown in sustainable forests. The logging
and manufacturing processes are expected to conform to the environmental
regulations of the country of origin.

Hachette Books Ireland
8 Castlecourt Centre
Castleknock
Dublin 15, Ireland

A division of Hachette UK Ltd
Carmelite House, 50 Victoria Embankment, London EC4Y 0DZ

www.hachettebooksireland.ie

CONTENTS

Some of the names and details within
this book have been changed.

*To all the women and children who
suffered injustices in Ireland, especially to
Joan, Terri, Deirdre and their families.*

AUTHOR'S NOTE

The scenes recreated in this book come directly from interviews with the contributors, portrayed to the best of their memories. As much as possible, I have included dialogue as quoted to me verbatim in interviews, but when it was not, I have deduced it from the contributors' descriptions of events. Some names and details have been changed to respect the privacy of individuals. Where names have been changed they have been marked with an asterisk.

Prologue

MAYO, JULY 2021

For the past two years, I've kept a photo on my desk of a three-storey Georgian mansion I have never been inside. This is a recent photo, but it shows how the brown-grey walls and cut-stone windows have weathered the years well. The house dates back to 1760; it can be found at the end of a long tree-lined drive on an historic estate on the outskirts of Cork City. A red-painted oak door adds a splash of colour, otherwise it looks imposing, almost unwelcoming.

This is Bessborough House, and though I am not permitted to explore it, I have visited its leafy grounds, beside a drab industrial park in the Cork City suburbs. Once past the gates, a narrow road winds its way past a security hut, wide fields and a compact playground. These days the grounds host a centre for vulnerable families, but for many years, the house operated as one of Ireland's largest mother and baby institutions, run by the Sisters of the Sacred Hearts of Jesus and Mary. The women and girls who passed through these doors had their children taken from them and placed for adoption, often without their consent.

By the time I came to hear the stories of those who passed through this house, I had been living outside of Ireland for many years working as a journalist for the BBC. In late 2017, I had returned from a stint as a producer in the Washington bureau with speech peppered with Americanisms and a desire to break away from a frantic news cycle. The world of 5 a.m. tweets and snarky soundbites had exhausted me; I longed to focus on longer-term projects, hear stories told in quieter voices.

Around that time, important conversations were happening in the country of my birth. Ireland was celebrating centenaries of the events that marked the struggle towards an independent state: the 1916 Rising, the bitter War of Independence and the fight for women's suffrage. It was a time of reflection on why the hopes and promises of an independent Ireland had not been delivered for all its citizens; films, books and documentaries had been commissioned to examine why so many aspects of women's lives had been placed outside their control.

A referendum on overturning the country's controversial abortion ban had also been called and I was sent to cover the campaign for the BBC website. In 2018, as the votes were counted, I stood among crowds who cheered and cried in Dublin Castle as the eighth amendment to the constitution was repealed. Taoiseach Leo Varadkar spoke of a 'quiet revolution' that had taken place in the country. 'It's also a day when we say no more ... no more stigma as the veil of secrecy is lifted and no more isolation as the burden of shame is gone,' he told the crowds. But the legacy of Ireland's adoption system kept cropping up in conversations. 'It's our present and that's what keeps being forgotten,' a woman I interviewed told me, herself adopted from a mother and baby institution.

Her words stayed with me. I had known about these places; as a child I heard snippets of hushed conversations, remnants of an era I would never quite understand. As a journalist in London, I watched the film *Philomena* and was aware of the thousands of Irish children sent to the US; I had felt disgust and shame when a mass grave was discovered at a former mother and baby institution in Tuam, County Galway, just twenty miles from my hometown. But I had always thought of these institutions in a historical sense; there was no longer a place for them in the country I had grown up in, one which had granted me free university fees and had recently legalised same-sex marriage. 'I get upset when people say that,' the actress and playwright Noelle Browne, adopted from the Bessborough institution, told me. 'It's not a new Ireland for me or 100,000 other people,' she said, referring to the approximate number of adoptees who passed through the Irish system, some of whom still face difficulty accessing their early-life files.

Later that year, I was commissioned by the BBC to write an article on the Commission of Investigation into Mother and Baby Homes underway at the time. I read the limited historical literature available, pored over yellowed documents and old photographs, and visited the sites of former homes, trying to understand their complicated legacy. It was not a task for the fainthearted; the religious orders responsible for running the homes declined interviews and some documents in state archives were inaccessible.

It took time to get in touch with survivors who felt ready to talk. Some, like Maura* from Connemara, wished to speak to me under a pseudonym. On a crackling phone line, she recounted how she had given birth to her first child in a mother and baby institution in the early 1980s. Her voice faltering in places, she told me I was one of the few people outside of her own family she had told about her time there. 'You blame yourself,' she said of keeping that secret bottled up. 'I always thought I was the only one in the world.' Others, like Noelle Browne, were less reticent; they spoke of the years they had spent battling to trace relatives and access personal information. 'The damage and the hurt are continuing into the present day,' Noelle explained.

While mother and baby institutions in other countries had closed their doors by the 1970s, Bessborough, where Noelle was born, remained in operation until the late 1990s. Almost 10,000 women passed through its doors between 1922 and 1998, and almost 9,000 children were born or admitted there. A group of five people, including mothers who had given birth in the institution and people adopted from there, spoke to me for a 5,000-word article published on the front page of the BBC news website in April 2019. It had been a surprise addition to the Chartbeat list of the most-read news articles in the world that year, performing well with audiences across the globe. The courage of the contributors had struck a chord with readers and prompted lots of people to get in touch and express their shock at the ways in which people were still affected.

Some of the messages came from people asking for information about support and advocacy groups. Others wrote about their personal experiences. Bernie* said: 'It has re-kindled my long-held (very secret) wish to uncover the circumstances of my birth ... I hope that it inspires other people, especially the children of these institutions, to demand answers.' Margaret* wrote to tell me about her mother, who had given birth in the home in the 1960s. Jim* told me about his wife's sister, sent to Bessborough in 1980 'to avoid scandal' where she was living under an assumed name in conditions he and his wife found unacceptable. The couple invited her to live with them. Debbie* wrote for help on behalf of her brother-in-law, who had been adopted from Ireland in the 1960s and couldn't find documents to prove his identity.

Alongside all of these messages was an email from a publisher who had spotted the piece; they wanted to explore the possibility of extending the article into a book focusing on a group of people from the Bessborough institution. As I read it, I doubted whether what they were proposing was possible. All of the contributors, people I had come to know and respect, had shared their experiences at huge personal cost to themselves. For some, taking part in a BBC article had been a great challenge. But most responded positively when I phoned them about the proposal: they saw it as an opportunity to bring the story of Bessborough to a wider audience.

As the weeks and months went on, I spoke with three women who expressed a willingness to share their stories publicly and who did not wish to hold anything back. To learn more about them, I have spoken with them many times over Skype and WhatsApp, have drunk cups of tea in their homes and have seen, where possible, their photos and personal documents relating to the institution. Their vivid accounts took me inside the walls of Bessborough House from the 1960s to the 1980s; through their eyes, we see the hastily packed cases in long-roomed dormitories; the pale walls of the downstairs delivery room; the nurseries filled with babies women and girls would never take home.

Seventy-four-year-old Joan McDermott was the first to sign up fully to this project. A tall, no-nonsense former nurse and social worker, she greeted me with a huge smile and freshly blow-dried blonde hair when I arrived to visit her at her home in Cork. Her blue eyeliner and gold shoes revealed a love of colourful things and inside her spotless kitchen she passed slice after slice of homemade rhubarb tart across the table. Joan urged me to 'put the bit of humour' in the chapters based on her experiences; an effusive talker, she could speak uninterrupted for an hour at a stretch. But for forty-six years she told no one about her experience of entering Bessborough as a teenage girl in 1967 and losing her child. 'Emotionally, I withdrew into myself,' she said of that time, puffing occasionally on her purple vape pen. 'I carried that all these years.' When she tried to trace her son, she encountered years of delays and difficulties that complicated her search. Over the past five years, she has met others sent there in the 1960s and early 1970s, when admissions were at their peak; some of their stories are also threaded throughout this book.

Coronavirus delayed my first meeting with sixty-seven-year-old Terri Harrison. Our conversations progressed from texts she sprinkled with pink heart emojis to WhatsApp calls where she spoke at length about her experiences.

Repatriated to Ireland from the UK, Terri entered Bessborough in 1973 as a pregnant eighteen-year-old with very little knowledge about sex. Her son was placed for adoption and she later married, reared three other children and went back to education in her forties, earning a degree. But she always felt as though she lived her life in a bubble, mourning the son she wasn't allowed to keep. 'I was lost in this horrible void that never went away ... I did a lot of stuff in silence and nobody knew,' she told me from her home in north Dublin. Despite a spell of ill health, the petite auburn-haired woman with a throaty laugh is an active campaigner. It's her way of dealing with what she calls 'a living bereavement'. 'The best I can do is learn how to cope ... it never stops.'

By the 1980s, conditions were better and more women were deciding to keep their children but many still felt pressured into adoptions. Deirdre Wadding's parents sent her to Bessborough in 1981; a cherished child from an aspirational family in County Wexford, she became pregnant as a student in Dublin. 'I lost every sense of myself,' she recalled, remembering the 'horrible, hurtful, abusive things' that were said to her. Even in the eighties, she didn't feel that she could challenge them about sending her to Bessborough. 'We believed we couldn't leave there,' she explained. 'That was how society worked.' Now in her fifties, with salt-and-pepper hair and a small silver nose stud, she is among the youngest surviving women to have given birth in a mother and baby institution. 'It's a life sentence,' she told me as she smoked a rollie by the front door of her rural cottage, her turquoise ring catching the autumn light.

Though their lives after Bessborough were shaped by their time there, Joan, Terri and Deirdre have all – in their own individual ways – refused to let their experience define them. I am incredibly grateful for the time they have spent with me, even when it was painful to look back at the past. Throughout the research for this book, never once did they shy away from questions, refuse to answer emails, express impatience at fact-checking or lose trust in the project. In the case of Joan and Deirdre, the sons placed for adoption prefer to keep a low profile and were not interviewed for this book. All three women expressed a desire for those affected to be given access to their records and spoke out in the wish that their experiences would never again happen to others. I hope the finished book honours the faith they have placed in me.

In January 2021, the Commission of Investigation into Mother and Baby Homes released its final report of a five-year inquiry. It found that about 15 per cent of infants born in the institutions examined by the commission died. 'In the years before 1960 mother and baby homes did not save the lives of "illegitimate" children; in fact, they appear to have significantly reduced their prospects of survival,' it concluded in its executive summary. The report revealed that in the seventy-six years Bessborough was in operation, 923 children born there died and it is not known where most of them are buried. The inquiry found 'no evidence' of forced adoption, while also recognising that the women and girls confined in these institutions would have had no choice but to give up their children. The report's findings – and Joan, Terri and Deirdre's responses to them – will be dealt with in the concluding chapter of this book.

As I compiled this mansucript, I returned many times to the photo on my desk of Bessborough House; its thick brown-grey walls have enclosed over seven decades of secrets. Writing about it has challenged what I thought I knew about the country of my birth and the state that was created after independence – a state that confined a higher number of pregnant women and girls in institutions than any other country in the world in the twentieth century. This book does not attempt to be a complete history of the Bessborough institution or of the system of adoption in Ireland; like the photo on my desk, it's a snapshot of a previous era through the eyes of a group of women who lived through it. They are not alone in their experiences but the accounts that follow are uniquely theirs.

Part One

JOAN'S STORY

Chapter One

CORK, 1967

Joan's mother and stepfather didn't say a word to her in the car. Kathleen* touched up her already red lips and brushed back a stray strand of her curly blonde hair. John* kept his eyes firmly on the road. Joan sat in the back, her stomach in knots, looking out the window of the family's Ford car. On another day she might have appreciated the view, the morning sunlight giving a soft glow to the high ridges of the Galtee Mountains that she knew so well. Today, though, it couldn't distract her from the tense feeling she hadn't been able to shake off since the day before. As night turned to morning, she'd lain awake, her mind going over and over the heated conversations she'd had with Kathleen.

'Where am I going?' she asked.

More silence. Joan kept her eyes on the road, watching the route. About an hour had passed since they had set off from the family home in Mitchelstown. They had driven by Fermoy and by the Blackwater River, and it seemed to Joan as they passed acres of well-tended farmland and busy market towns that they were heading in the direction of Cork City.

The car turned onto a country road in the suburbs, slowing to stop outside a set of wrought-iron gates which opened to reveal a wide avenue. At the top was a three-storey Georgian mansion partially shielded from view with shrubs and trees. Joan could tell it had once been grand – two stone pillars in the shape of lions framed the front steps and there was an old glass conservatory with curved windows to the side. The front door was painted a glossy red and the lawns and flowerbeds were neatly trimmed.

'Out you get,' said Kathleen.

Joan grabbed her overnight bag, where she'd stuffed a change of clothes the night before. Taking a deep breath, she made her way up the stone steps. As the door swung open, she could hear Kathleen and John heading back to the car, then the crunch of the wheels on the gravel.

Here goes, she thought, taking a step forward into the house.

Chapter Two

CORK, 1966

Joan and Ellen* clamoured for a space around the cracked mirror in the tennis club changing room. A sticky cloud of hairspray and chemist shop perfume made them cough. 'Quick, pass me the lipstick', Joan instructed Ellen, who dutifully handed it over. Joan dotted the peach-pink shade on her lips, fixed her dark curls in place and gestured for Ellen to follow her towards the door. 'Come on, we'll miss the first dance,' she told her.

'He's looking at you again,' said Ellen, giving her a nudge as they approached the dance floor. Joan knew who she meant: his name was Ben*, she knew that much, he was a couple of years older and a law student at UCC. She'd heard some of the college girls talk about him in the bathrooms.

'Are you sure it's me?'

'I'm telling you, it's definitely you.' Ellen nudged her again and pushed her forward.

'Dance?' he said. Joan felt her cheeks flush. Up close, Ben was even more handsome than she thought: tall, clear-skinned, with dark-blond hair. She turned her head to see if he meant another girl standing behind her, but she couldn't see anyone.

'Go on so,' she said, taking his hand as he led her over to the floor.

'I'm Ben. Nice to meet you.'

'Joan,' she replied, following his steps.

'Are you friends with Rose*?'

'Rose invited me.'

Joan's hand fitted easily in his for The Beach Boys and the set-dance tracks, and his hands remained respectfully around her waist even during the lull of the slow tunes. When the lights flickered on and the crowd stood for the national anthem at midnight, she saw that his eyes were a pale shade of blue.

'Thanks for a lovely time,' he said. 'Would you, maybe ... like to do this again sometime?'

'Yes. Lovely. That would be lovely,' she replied, wondering if he'd noticed that she'd said it a tad too hastily.

From across the room, Ellen gave her a knowing look and Joan suspected it might be the start of her very first romance.

❖

Their first date was at the pictures. That morning, Joan couldn't touch her breakfast, or her lunch, wondering whether it would be better to wear another tea dress or a skirt and blouse. She'd ask him questions about his friends, his degree, his family. If the conversation dried up, she'd tell him about her plans to be a vet, if her exam results were good enough.

'You look nice,' he told her when he saw her outside the picture house.

Joan thought the same about him; he looked freshly shaved, with a neatly ironed shirt and a discreet smell of upmarket cologne. The conversation flowed. He had a big family, lots of brothers, he was enjoying his law degree and to Joan he seemed so clever.

Joan loved the cinema, but sitting beside Ben, she couldn't pay attention to the plot; she felt giddy in his company. Each time he moved in his seat, she wondered, or rather worried, if he was going to kiss her; if he didn't, she wouldn't have anything to tell Ellen about, and if he did, she wasn't sure how she should respond. When his lips finally met hers, it was brief but wonderful too in its own way.

Joan was smitten. Within a few weeks they were an item. Ben's family were wealthy like Joan's: they owned a thriving business on the outskirts of Cork City. He was the first in his family to go to university and had his own car, a black Mini. On a Sunday afternoon, he would collect her and they'd go for a drive and take a picnic, not returning until late in the evening. Or they'd take a boat from Crosshaven all the way out to Cobh, watching the sun shimmering over the water. And in the evening they'd have dinner with his brothers and their girlfriends in a restaurant overlooking the harbour.

Joan could tell Ben anything – he was respectful, kind, someone to confide in. She told him that even though her grades hadn't been the best the year before, she still thought she'd like to go to university and be a vet. She told him how her mother had tried so hard to get her to be more ladylike, but even now her favourite thing to do was to play a hockey match in the mud. Or how she loved playing the piano but hated when her mother wanted her to entertain the group of women she invited over for afternoon tea.

And she told him the serious stuff too; he knew that after her father had slipped into a diabetic coma and died when she was sixteen, she hadn't been the same since. He knew too that her mother packed her off to boarding school when she was ten, telling her to 'for goodness' sake get on that train', and never visited her. She told him how with each year that passed, she'd felt a stranger in her family home when she returned for the holidays. Ben knew all of this, and still arrived the next Sunday to pick her up.

After every date, she counted down the days until the next one, remembering every detail to tell Ellen about later. As the summer came to an end and a soft chill crept into the August evenings, she felt her stomach fill with dread as she took the trip to Dublin to be fitted for her replacement uniform.

'I guess I'll see you when I'm home for a visit,' she told Ben on their final date of the summer. It was her final year in the boarding school and her exams were coming up. Maybe the days would pass quickly, like Ben had said. Or maybe they wouldn't, maybe they'd pass so slowly she wouldn't be able to bear it. There was little chance she could write to him – the nuns vetted everything and a sneaky letter to a boyfriend would be extracted from the pile before it even reached the postbox.

Chapter Three

CORK, 1967

Kathleen sat in the armchair by the small table in the drawing room. Her face was pale.

'How could you, Joan? How could you be so reckless?'

'I didn't mean to—'

'I presume Ben is the father?'

'Yes.'

Kathleen had discovered Joan retching over the bathroom sink and had whisked her off to an appointment. From the moment they had emerged from the doctor's surgery with the news that Joan was indeed pregnant, she had quizzed Joan non-stop, barely pausing to take a breath.

'This doesn't happen to girls like you,' she continued. 'Girls from good families and good schools. You're not a servant girl or a maid. And how is this going to look for me and your stepfather? Did you think about that?'

Joan thought of the parties her mother threw for other wealthy families in the area, solicitors and politicians and businessmen and their wives. How Kathleen would hate to be on the wrong side of the local rumour mill.

'But—'

It had been almost an hour and Joan had struggled to utter even a syllable. She shifted uncomfortably from foot to foot on the red Persian-style rug in the middle of the floor. The drawing room was her mother's domain, and Joan always felt like an intruder there.

'Is he going to marry you?' She didn't wait for Joan to respond, making a gesture to dismiss her.

Joan's cheeks burned. When her period hadn't arrived the first month, she hadn't given it a second thought, and even when she'd missed the second, she still hadn't put two and two together. She'd only ever had whispered conversations about these things with friends from the tennis club, and biology class gave a rudimentary mention of the menstrual cycle and little else. There had been just two incidents with Ben when she'd been back home during the school term and she had never imagined it would lead to this. Her mother had kept using that word, illegitimate. And her tone towards her, Joan hated it, it made her feel ashamed.

She phoned Ben from the house phone downstairs. The news felt all the more scary and real when she spoke the words out loud.

'Right', he said. There was a pause. It was too long for Joan's liking. 'Okay. Right.' Another pause followed, more awkward than the first one. 'I have a lot of things to think about. My degree for a start ... and I can't tell my mother. You know she's been on her own since my father died. This would just totally destroy her.'

His tone worried Joan. He seemed very far away, not like the Ben who had been her boyfriend for two summers in a row.

'But Ben—'

He gave a deep sigh. 'There's nothing I can do about it, Joan – you'll have to go to England.'

Footsteps. Her mother grabbed the receiver and shooed Joan out.

'You're the one responsible for this. What are you going to do about it?' Joan heard her mother say. The door closed behind her before she could hear any more.

That night, Joan lay awake staring at the pink and white speckled wallpaper in her bedroom, watching as the hours passed and cracks of light started to come in through the grooves in the white shutters. A baby was going to arrive in a few months' time, that was certain. But how was she going to get Kathleen to calm down? This hadn't happened to anyone she knew, not at boarding school, not to anyone she knew from the tennis club dances. And Ben had been so strange. What did he mean about going to England? Would he come round or phone her up to apologise?

A tight feeling formed in her chest. From her bedroom she heard little but she imagined the long conversation that Kathleen and John were having, about actions, consequences, the right thing to do. They'd probably progressed from cups of tea to tumblers of whiskey, making decisions about how to deal with things without any input from her. She thought of her father – what would he have said if he had been alive to see it? Would he too have looked at her as though she had let him down?

The next morning Kathleen appeared in the doorway of Joan's bedroom; her eyes wouldn't meet Joan's.

'Put some clothes in a bag and be ready to leave in an hour.'

'Where am I going?' Joan asked.

'You'll find out soon enough.'

Chapter Four

BESSBOROUGH, 1967

The nun who opened the door to Joan didn't smile or greet her by name but instead surveyed her with a cool stare. She wore a loose black habit with a stiff veil and gestured for Joan to follow. Inside the house, Joan could see a long, wide corridor with a gleaming parquet floor, doors and panels made of dark wood and a huge wooden staircase. Her throat tickled from the smell of furniture polish. With short, quick footsteps, the nun led her up three flights of stairs to the top floor.

'Your mother and stepfather have told me all about your situation.'

Joan nodded. Best not to say very much, she thought.

'Is there a name you would like to be called while you are in the house? No one uses their real name here.'

Joan stumbled. 'No, I mean ...'

'In that case, your house name is Michelle. You will answer to this name from now on. And you will say you are from Limerick, not from Mitchelstown. When you leave here you can tell people you were on a nursing course in England and decided to come back.' She paused, as if gauging Joan's reaction. 'This will be yours,' she said, indicating a small single bed. 'Dinner will be served at six and the others will show you where to go. There are three main rules of this house and you would do well to adhere to them:

'Do not reveal your identity to any other girl.

'You are to have no contact with the outside world.

'If you run away, you will be brought back by the police.'

Left alone, Joan surveyed her sparse, spotless surroundings. The dormitories had once been long – perhaps even elegant – rooms, now partitioned; in Joan's section, there were four beds with crisp sheets tightly tucked in at the edges. The only other furnishings were some bedside lockers and a single crucifix on the pale green walls. On the bed was a starched blue dress which she guessed was her uniform; she wondered how long she would have to wear it before she could go back home. She changed quickly, stuffing her dress and overnight bag into the locker. The tunic was shapeless, made of a rough, denim-like material that had faded to a washed-out colour over the years. She sighed. If her mother and stepfather had wanted to teach her a lesson, sending her here seemed like a bizarre way of doing it.

She heard the sound of the floors squeaking under rubber shoes as a group of three girls arrived to wash their hands. She guessed that they were in their late teens like herself, and all were in different stages of pregnancy. None met her eyes or made much of an effort to acknowledge her, apart from one girl, with mousy brown hair, about Joan's age. 'I'm Julia,' she said, with a weak smile. 'Or at least that's what they call me in here.'

Joan stumbled. 'Michelle. I'm from Limerick.' The words tumbled awkwardly from her mouth; they sounded ridiculous in her Cork accent.

'Follow me, it's time for dinner.'

Joan followed the girls downstairs, taking in the house's high ceilings and a stained-glass window. On the ground floor, Julia pointed out a parlour, an office and a reception room, but Joan didn't get a chance to see inside any of them. As the door opened into the dining room, Joan heard the clanging of plates echoing off the walls. A group of around twenty young women sat around in small groups at wooden tables laid with white crockery, mostly in silence, whispering when they did speak. The meal was bland, the sort of institutional stew she was used to getting at boarding school. Joan couldn't touch it. At the top of the room another of the nuns read passages from a leather-bound Bible in a loud voice. Some words got particular emphasis: Stained. Repentance. Shame.

That night, as Joan lay awake, she heard muffled crying through the partitions. 'How long have you been here?' she whispered to Julia, who slept in the next bed.

'Three months now. I can't wait to get out. The girl that was in the bed before you had her baby so she was moved to another section of the home. We'll go there too when our time comes.'

'When do you get out?'

'When you have the baby. But until then you're stuck here.'

Joan turned her head over onto the cool side of the pillow, exhausted. She couldn't bring herself to ask any more questions. She had a feeling she wouldn't like the answers.

The next morning, Joan woke early, just after 6 a.m., to the sound of a bell. For a moment, she didn't understand where she was, but when she did, the realisation did little to relieve the knots in her stomach. She joined the queue that had formed at the hand basins in the bathrooms and washed and dressed quickly.

'We have mass before we eat,' explained Julia.

The service began at 7 a.m. in a large downstairs room smelling of incense and candles that was used as a chapel. The girls sat at the front in long wooden pews with the nuns in a row behind them. A priest lectured them on penance, sacrifice and the sins of the flesh, his vestments the only dash of colour among the girls' faded uniforms and the nuns' habits. At breakfast, Joan sat beside Julia, trying her best to eat the sticky porridge and whispering to her when she could. She noticed something she hadn't seen the day before, that some of the women there were older than her and Julia, perhaps in their forties or maybe more.

'Why are they still here?' she whispered.

'They had their children here a long time ago. They never left.'

'Why not? Surely they wouldn't want to stay here if they didn't have to.'

'Nobody really knows. Maybe their families didn't want them back? They work in the kitchens now.'

Joan set aside her spoon. She didn't much feel like eating any more.

'What do we do for the rest of the day?'

'You have to work. One of the nuns will tell you where to go. It can be in the kitchens, outside on the farm or in the nursery on the first floor with the babies. Or there's gardening too, weeding and cutting grass. If you're really unlucky, in the laundry with me. The steam is the worst.'

Joan imagined a dark building with a huge machine, a wringer and lines of wet, soggy sheets and silently hoped she didn't end up there. The bell clanged again at 8 a.m., and Julia mouthed a silent good luck to Joan.

'Michelle, isn't it?' said a nun she hadn't seen before. 'You're to go out in the gardens,' she told her, before Joan had a chance to respond. She pointed her towards a line of about eight girls filing out of the dining hall. Outside, Joan breathed a sigh of relief. It was warmer in the gardens than inside the house; maybe in the fresh air, the heavy feeling in her chest might start to subside.

The grounds were immaculately kept, with tidy lawns and neatly trimmed flowerbeds, the rose bushes full of late summer blooms. To the right, Joan could see a small, clear lake, glistening in the weak sun, and heard some cows roaming the farm.

'You and Mary can work together,' said the nun.

The other girl was about twenty, with long blonde hair and a shy smile. When she introduced herself, Joan could hear the soft lilt of a Donegal accent.

The nun opened a box of kitchen scissors.

'Off you go, let's start on the front lawns today,' she said.

Joan tried to catch Mary's eye. Did she really expect them

to cut the lawn with scissors? But Mary just gave her a meaningful look and started cutting. Joan stood for a second, before Mary gave her a nudge and Joan took her place beside her. On their hands and knees, they tackled small sections, putting the cuttings into small cotton bags, not progressing to the next section until the nun inspected the patch and nodded her approval. Piece by piece, they trimmed the lawn, cutting away the long blades as if restoring a precious painting.

At noon, the girls were ushered back into the dining room for a lunch of soup. Joan couldn't work out what vegetable it tasted of but tried her best to eat it; it was difficult to distinguish it from the stew that had been served the night before. Then they returned to their duties until it was time for dinner.

At 6 p.m., Joan followed the girls into a downstairs room they called the dayroom. It wasn't comfortable, with its rows of hard bench tables that reminded Joan of her days in the convent boarding school, and there was no television or non-holy books to distract them. Some of the girls were knitting baby clothes; Joan could make out shapes that might become bootees or matinee cardigans.

What are you knitting? she wanted to say.

'Clack' went the needles as the words remained stuck in her throat.

Why were they being punished like this? she wanted to ask. When could she go back home? She took a deep breath and sat up straight but the words wouldn't come. The clacking continued until seven and no one really made any attempt at small talk.

You're on your own here, Joan thought as she made her way upstairs for the night. You'd better get used to it.

Chapter Five

BESSBOROUGH, 1967

'What would it be like if I got to keep the baby?' Joan whispered to Julia.

She wasn't sure whether the other girl would be awake. It was a few hours after lights out, and only the shadowy outlines of the other beds were visible. From the next bed, Julia's response was muffled.

'Sometimes I let myself get carried away,' she said. 'I think about how nice it would be to go home with a little boy or girl and my parents would be grandparents ... I could go for a walk with the baby in the pram and show all my friends ... But then I remember how angry my mam and dad were and I put my head down and get on with things.'

'Mine were so furious. I'd never seen my mother that angry with me before. But I still keep hoping she'll change her mind and come and collect me with my stepfather.'

'I know for a fact that my family don't want anything to do with me or the baby.' Julia sighed. 'The only way for me to keep mine is to go to England. But I don't know anyone there, and what kind of job would I be able to get anyway? I can't wait to get out of here and put all of this behind me.'

Joan hadn't had a visitor or received a letter from anyone in the months she'd been in the home, and she'd started to lose hope that her mother and stepfather might come and collect her. The schedule of mass and work meant she hardly ever spoke to anyone else, so these rare whispered conversations in the dark made things feel less lonely. Joan had told her all about Ben, and in turn she had heard the stories about Julia's boyfriend, a farmer's son from the country. Sometimes Julia told her about the stories she had heard about girls who had been there before them; there was the girl whose cousin had had his way with her; others who had one encounter at the seaside and had ended up in Bessborough; another who'd had an affair with a married man. Like Joan, they had little idea of how babies were made, just the little bits of knowledge they had passed down from older sisters or cousins or friends. And there were the rumours about the girls who had married the father of the child and returned to their hometowns with their babies, respectability restored.

Joan had long grown weary of long days that merged into one. The attitude of the nuns here was so different to those at her boarding school. In Roscrea, they had kept a teacherly distance, and irritated Joan with their obsession with manners and rules, but they weren't unkind. Here they seemed to think the very worst of Joan and it didn't appear likely to change. She had barely spoken to them, barely knew any of their names, but she'd lost count of the number of times she'd heard that she deserved what had happened to her, that she'd sinned, and was a lost soul. 'You'll go out into the world, but you'll never make anything of yourself because of what you did. No man will ever marry you, so resign yourself to the fact you'll never have a family because you're unclean.' When one of the other girls had suggested that she might keep her child, a nun had scoffed at the suggestion. 'Get that idea out of your head,' she'd said to the unwitting girl. 'There are lots of respectable families lining up to take the children and they'll be far better off with them. And you won't be allowed to search for them either; you won't ever be able find them again.'

The question about what would happen to her own child overshadowed all of Joan's thoughts. She'd tried to put it out of her mind, but as the weeks passed and she felt the baby grow bigger, it was impossible not to think about the birth. In just three more months, the baby would arrive and she would see its face, touch the feet that jabbed against her ribs. Surely she wouldn't have to give him or her away? Her mother and stepfather were angry with her, yes, but they weren't short of a few bob and once they saw their grandchild surely they'd want to take the baby home?

Other things troubled her. Just a couple of days ago, she had heard the sound of soft crying from the other end of the dining table. At first she didn't dare glance in the direction of the sound, keeping her eyes on that day's variation of the lunchtime vegetable soup. The situation made Joan nervous; she willed the girl to gather herself.

'Quiet,' came the voice of one of the nuns.

When Joan finally craned her head to look, a few minutes later, it was a girl she didn't know. The sound continued to echo across the dining hall until two nuns stood either side of the girl and administered an injection into her arm.

'Come on, Joan, we should go to sleep now. There's no point thinking too much about things,' Julia whispered.

Their conversations always ended up like this, going around and around in a circle of unanswered questions until both girls decided there was no point in continuing. Joan pulled the sheets around herself. Julia was right. Sometimes, it was best not to ponder things too deeply.

❖

In the morning, Joan couldn't stop yawning. Her eyes were heavy with sleep as she tried to focus on the flowerbeds and lawns. The occasional mooing of the cows made her think of the farm visits she had accompanied her father on when he was still alive. She would climb into the back of the Ford car alongside his veterinary bag, pleading with him to take her along. 'I want to see the animals being born,' she would beg. He would laugh like he always did, giving a permissive shake of his head, and Joan would feel a familiar contentment as they drove to the manor houses with dairy farms and stables, then across twisty mountain lanes to the whitewashed cottages with a lean-to for the pigs and chickens running in through the half door.

Joan would watch in half horror and half astonishment as her father pulled out fluid-soaked baby calves from their mothers. It didn't bother him to drink tea from rusty tin cups or to accept payment in eggs, rather than cash, from families eking out a living on the harsh mountain soil. 'Never think you are better than anybody else,' he would tell her. 'You are who you are. Treat everybody with respect.' If he had still been around, would she have ended up here? Would he have stood up for her?

Mary's soft voice interrupted her thoughts. 'Joan, you look tired. They're at a prayer meeting. You don't have to worry too much about the weeding today. But you're in another world anyway.'

'I couldn't sleep. Thinking about things.'

'That makes two of us. I keep thinking about my son. He's so adorable, Joan, his name's Liam and if you saw him you'd love him, and he's learning to talk now. But I can't leave until I know they've found a good home for him. He's two now and the others were all adopted as babies. I don't want him to end up in an orphanage.'

'Why is he still here?'

'His father was an African student; I met him in Dublin. He was from Nigeria, and then, well … it's the same story as yours. The nuns said it's very hard to find a couple who will take him on. But I don't want Liam to grow up without a family.'

Joan nodded. It was difficult to find anything comforting to say.

Mary gave a quick glance around the garden. 'Come on, they won't be back for a while yet. I'll show you where he is.'

Grabbing Joan's hand, Mary led her upstairs to the first floor, past the nursery and to a locked door in part of the house normally forbidden.

'In here,' she said, knocking on the heavy wooden door.

When it opened, Joan could see a large, sparse room with green walls and rows and rows of iron cots. Inside, about fifteen toddlers were being looked after by an older woman, whom Joan hadn't seen before. Mary pointed out Liam, a small, delicate child with round brown eyes and curly dark hair. He was gorgeous, exactly as Mary had said. Some of the children had disabilities and others were mixed race like Liam. The older ones stood in their cots, clinging to the bars, and some held their hands out to the girls, begging to be picked up.

'I try to come up as often as I can,' Mary said, 'but thinking about him being left here, it upsets me. They said he was unadoptable.'

Joan felt her breath catch in her throat. 'I'm so sorry, Mary,' she said.

But Mary hadn't heard her, she'd gone straight to Liam and given him a little hug, before the two girls made their way downstairs in silence. Joan thought of her own baby, a bundle that moved and jumped and kicked, and she shuddered to think what might happen if he or she was deemed unsuitable for adoption.

As autumn approached and the leaves began to clutter the walkways, Joan started to feel as though her mind was in a different place, that things would happen around her in a way that she was entirely disconnected from. She looked forward to the moment when the lights went out in the dormitory and she could fall into a deep sleep; when she woke, she didn't draw attention to herself, spoke less and less to the other girls.

The weeks came and went, and when the tress grew bare, those on gardening duties were brought back in and assigned cleaning duties. Inside, Joan always felt cold in the draughty corridors and missed the fresh air of the garden. Even in the final weeks of her pregnancy, there was little respite from hard work. She scrubbed every inch of the faded parquet floors with a bucket of soapy water and a stiff bristled brush until her hands were raw. All of her energy and fury were poured into that floor.

Chapter Six

BESSBOROUGH, 1967

The day after St Stephen's Day, Joan put down her bristle brush and sat up. Her back twinged, had hurt since morning. It was an unfamiliar sensation, but she wondered if it might pass. She dipped the brush back into the bucket but the discomfort continued.

'Please, I want to take something for the pain,' she asked the nun in charge.

'Just get back to your work.'

All through the rest of the day, the pain continued to progress. Could this be it? Could she be in labour? Maybe it was nothing – other girls had had false alarms and then had to wait weeks before their babies had arrived. And it wasn't as if she could ask anyone; in the whole time she had been there, she hadn't seen a doctor or a midwife. When she'd first arrived, she'd had to give blood and urine samples but when she'd tried to find out what they were for, the woman taking them had ignored her.[1]

In bed that evening, Joan couldn't settle – she felt agitated, a tugging pain beginning in her abdomen. Her waters broke, the warm fluid reminding her that the situation was outside of her control. The pain intensified and she shuffled downstairs, almost bent double with the pain, to tell the matron.

'Please, I'm in so much pain, can I have something?'

Unmoved, the matron led her into a tiny room. A small window behind the bed and another above the door allowed light in, and the room was just about long enough for a single bed and a commode wedged against the wall. Each end of the bed touched the wall and, looking at it, Joan understood why the girls had nicknamed it 'the cell'.

'You'll stay here until you're ready to deliver.'

Joan heard the click of the key in the lock as the door closed behind the matron, and she felt the panic start to rise in her throat. Surely they're not going to leave me in here on my own? she thought, as the minutes turned to hours and her eyes stung with hot tears. Through the night, the pains grew stronger and more frequent, a hard, gripping pain that came in waves. After a few hours, she saw the dawn light come in through the tiny window and she wondered if by the end of the day it would all be over.

Sometime after 8 a.m. the door opened.

'Please, just give me something for the pain,' she asked again, shouting at the matron this time.

'Absolutely not. You've done the devil's work. Get over here to this other room.'

Across the corridor, Joan could see the delivery room, bare except for a metal trolley with a sheet and a sink in the corner. Doubled over, she struggled to reach it and by the time she'd crossed the doorway there wasn't enough time to get up on the trolley. She leaned against it and with a final push the baby emerged. 'It's a boy,' said a voice she didn't recognise. There was a pause and Joan heard her son cry for the first time.

'It's all over, Joan, you can rest now.' It was the same voice, kind and calm.

Joan looked around for the baby, but he was immediately taken away. Exhausted, she was helped into a room with six beds where she fell into a deep sleep and woke up hours later, shivering and disorientated. The girl with the kind voice guided her into the bathroom to help her bathe. The feeling of the warm water was calming but Joan couldn't quite feel relieved.

'Who are you?'

'I'm Ann. I had my baby a couple of days ago. They send us in to help the next girl. Your son is in the nursery now,' she said, helping Joan back to bed. 'Just try to get some rest.'

A few hours later, Joan rushed to the nursery at feeding time. It was a large room on the first floor, with about twenty silver-painted cots on each side. On one side was a high window overlooking the grounds; on the other, a pair of glass doors. Like the rest of the building, it was painted a drab shade of institutional green, with no other colour except for a few grey tiles. At one end of the room, she saw a nun and another woman, who rumour had it had given birth in the home some years previously to a baby who'd subsequently died. Joan didn't know whether it was true.

Joan's son's cot was in the middle of the row on the left-hand side. He was wrapped in a blanket and, seeing him for the first time, his strong-featured face, his dark hair, his sturdy body, she felt a rush of pride. He weighed almost nine pounds, with a long body for a newborn. She wanted to call him David. As she listened to his gurgles and noises, she felt a wave of love for him that surprised her.

She followed the lead of the other mothers, picking him up and trying to get him to feed, which he seemed to know how to do instinctively. 'Face the wall and avoid eye contact,' the nun in charge told Joan. 'Don't expose your breast to the others.'

Joan knew better than to argue the point. After about thirty minutes, she and the others were shooed away.

'When can I see him again?' she asked the woman.

'At the next feed in a couple of hours.'

The glass doors were locked and Joan was again separated from her son.

Joan's body healed quickly. Every day, she counted down the hours, waiting for the next moment when she could feed her son, bathe him, change him and dress him. She loved his tiny fists and his robust baby body, which grew so fast she could almost see a change in him every day. She thought of her own mother, Kathleen, who she suspected hadn't felt the same way about her. Growing up, Bridie, the family's maid, was more of a mother figure to her than Kathleen. It was always Bridie who cared for her when she was sick, who told her stories and tucked her into bed at night as the stars shifted over a Golden Vale sky.

Sometimes, as she left the nursery, she could hear David crying on the other side of the glass, but she wasn't allowed in to comfort him. As the New Year came and went, Joan knew that trying not to feel anything for her baby boy was futile; it was already too late for that.

Chapter Seven

BESSBOROUGH, 1968

When Joan entered the parlour, she saw a room with heavy curtains, a mahogany dining table and chairs with leather seats. A decorative mirror hung over a marble fireplace and the late January sun streamed in through the large windows. Just like in the rest of the house, the floor was highly polished and Joan wondered which of the girls had been responsible for cleaning it. It took her a moment to register that her parents were sitting on the leather chairs, having tea and biscuits, and some of the more senior members of the order were present. She hung back.

'Joan. Come in,' the mother superior said to her. Her tone was warmer towards her in those three words than she had ever remembered it being in all her time in Bessborough.

Joan positioned herself beside the chair nearest the door. Her mother was dressed in an expensive two-piece and Joan got the familiar smell of Estée Lauder Youth Dew perfume. It had been her mother's fragrance of choice for years. Joan had never liked it – she found it sickly, heavy. She felt especially conscious of her shabby uniform.

'Mother, John, hello,' she said in a low voice. She wasn't sure whether she was to speak or not. 'How are you?' she asked.

'Your mother and stepfather have come here to discuss your future,' continued the reverend mother. 'I'll leave you to it,' she added, getting up from her chair.

'Hello, Joan, nice to see you.' John always tried to be affable – he liked to leave a good impression. Joan imagined that he had charmed the nuns with his repertoire of small talk. She'd always found it impressive, the amount of conversation he could generate without saying anything of consequence.

Her mother gave a curt nod. Joan was going to tell her about David, but seeing the cold expression on her face, she stopped herself.

As the weeks had passed, Joan had become more and more convinced that once Kathleen and John saw David they would fall in love with him like she had and would want to bring him home. Now, face to face with her mother, she felt less sure. But all she could do was try.

'Would you like to see your grandson?' she asked Kathleen. 'He's a few weeks old now and he's gorgeous. I could run upstairs and ask them to open the nursery and bring him down.'

'I've no interest in seeing a bastard child,' Kathleen replied. 'There was never a bastard born into our family until now.' Her tone wasn't angry, as it had been all those months ago; it had cooled to a sort of indifference that frightened Joan.

'But I want to keep him.'

'Nonsense, no illegitimate child is coming back to my house and that is that. You'll have to give him up, like the others.'

The reverend mother returned. 'You can go now, Joan, we need to speak to your parents.'

Joan turned to go, with a sinking feeling that she was powerless to stop a plan that had already been set in motion.

Two days later, Joan was in the nursery with David at feeding time when she heard the sound of quick footsteps approaching and the clink of rosary beads. A nun she didn't know lifted David from her arms and took him down a long corridor.

'Where are you taking him?' Joan said, running behind her.

The nun didn't respond.

'Stop,' Joan shouted. 'Bring him back.'

She heard the door sliding into place with a click as her son disappeared behind the frosted glass into the convent. She banged on the door, again and again, until one of the other girls ushered her away. For the rest of the morning, no one mentioned it. And in a way, Joan understood; it wouldn't be the last of these scenes and what use were their words anyway? They wouldn't bring David back.

In the afternoon, Joan returned to her cleaning duties as normal. When she saw the nun come back, she wanted to rush towards her, but she gathered herself, stifling the rage that was bubbling up inside her. What was the point anyway? It wasn't as if anyone cared what she thought. That night, in the dormitories, she cried softly to herself for the first time since she had arrived in Bessborough. Her breasts ached, despite the Epsom salt solution she'd been given; her body still thought she should be feeding David.

A few days later, Joan was again called downstairs. John and Kathleen stood outside the parlour door.

'Pack up quickly, we need to get going,' Kathleen said.

Back in the dormitory, Joan changed out of her uniform and pulled out the summer clothes and shoes that had been in the bedside locker for months. She'd only spent a few weeks with David, but in that time she'd seen him grow and develop, got to know his little sounds and gurgles. Now she was leaving the old house without him. She felt numb as she walked down the wooden staircase for the final time.

'Goodbye, sister,' said John, as one of the nuns opened the front door.

Joan got into the car without a word. But instead of heading north for home, they seemed instead to be travelling in the opposite direction.

'I'm not going home?' she asked.

On a freezing February afternoon, Joan was dropped at the airport, in her summer clothes and light jacket. There were no hugs or promises to write. In her hand was a ticket for the next flight to London.

Bessborough 1922–70

Joan has a loud voice, a thick Cork accent and likes to share memes from 'The Original Cranky Old Women Group'. Her interviews were full of colour and she often began our chats with an anecdote about how her week had been, like the time Coco the dog had five teeth removed and Joan had to nurse him back to health with pipettes of morphine. Quickly, though, the conversations would take a different turn. It was hard not to be affected by the harshness of what she experienced and her striking ability to remember Bessborough's smells, sights and sounds. Over the years, she'd lost any reticence about talking about her experience in a mother and baby institution. She was motivated, she told me, by a desire to speak out because others were either dead or not in a position to do so. 'It's our truth,' she told me. 'What kind of woman would I be if I could just cut off [from it]?' And at the end of some of our sessions, she asked me if I had found them hard to listen to, checking, to my shame, to see if I was alright rather than the other way around.

After each interview, I tried to find out more about the system of mother and baby institutions, shocked by how little I knew, how little I had been taught at school. I bought second-hand books, scoured library catalogues and read what I could online. I thought often of our conversations as I leafed through dusty volumes of government reports at a mahogany desk in Dublin's National Library. Every mention of Bessborough reminded me of Joan's descriptions; I remembered them as I took photographs of the yellowed entries on fragile paper, looked through newspaper archives and examined the reports of government commissions. The official sources will never capture the reality of her experience. But they do provide some insight into the cold system that separated children from their mothers and how it was administered.

Bessborough was one of the first mother and baby institutions to be set up in Ireland. Conversations about it began in 1921, when the matron of the Cork workhouse appealed to the Cork Board of Guardians to find alternative accommodation for unmarried mothers in the locality. Around that time, the idea had taken root in Ireland that single mothers should be separated from other people requiring government assistance. It was almost impossible for unmarried mothers to find a job or a place to live and officials believed that they should be accommodated in institutions run by religious orders, with an emphasis on moral salvation. Catholic clerics feared that if services were not improved, women would turn to Protestant rescue societies and that their children would be lost to the Catholic faith. Reading through old journals from that time, there are plenty of references to 'unfortunate girls' who turned in 'desperation' to Protestant agencies, who were 'only too ready' to receive them.[2]

The Board of Guardians invited an English congregation, the Sisters of the Sacred Hearts of Jesus and Mary, who were running a Catholic mother and baby institution in Highgate, London, to come to Cork. The board identified Bessborough House, a large Georgian house overlooking the River Lee, as a suitable location. Helped by a contribution from the archbishop of Westminster, the congregation bought the house, 210-acre site and accompanying farm buildings in 1922. The first women and children were admitted in November of that year. From the outset, the congregation was responsible for maintaining the estate and paying staff but the institution received public funding from the local health authorities and was inspected by the state.

Bessborough was seen as a sort of prototype, a blueprint for other institutions that would later be established to accommodate unmarried women and their children in the independent Free State, established just weeks after Bessborough opened its doors. The institution was intended as a 'special home' for Catholic women and girls, designed for 'young mothers who have fallen for the first time and who are likely to return to a useful and respectable life', according to a Department of Local Government and Public Health report from 1928–9. The sixty-five mothers who had been admitted to Bessborough that year were 'trained in domestic work, poultry-keeping and gardening'. The women and girls – who came from Cork, Kilkenny, Waterford, Tipperary and Kerry – were 'instructed in their religion' and 'provided with a suitable situation' or found a domestic job when they left the home. Local authorities paid for the cost of maintaining the women and girls in the institution, and children were 'boarded out' in informal foster arrangements.

There were never legal powers to detain women and girls in any such institution. But the language used in official documents sometimes linked them with criminal behaviour. 'First offenders' were deemed to be capable of reform, to be treated with 'firmness', 'discipline', but also 'charity' and 'sympathy', as outlined in a local government report from 1927, but those 'who had fallen more than once' were deemed 'less hopeful cases'. In 1930, the matron, Sr Martina, told government inspectors that 'a number of the girls are weak-willed and have to be maintained in the Home for a long period to safeguard them against a second lapse'.

In the early years, women and girls were admitted to Bessborough only after giving birth. They were given a 'house name' and spent an average of three years in the home, while their children could spend two, three or even five years or more there. I was reminded of Joan's descriptions of older women when I read about the eleven 'old girls', as they were referred to in government reports. They entered the home in the 1920s and never left, even after their children died or were boarded out. I could not find any trace of their voices on official documents: we may never know their full stories and those of their children. One woman, who entered in 1924, died there in 1985, most of her adult life spent behind the walls of the Bessborough institution.

Admissions increased in the 1930s, when a maternity ward was opened, followed by the Sacred Heart Maternity Hospital which was built on the site in 1934. The institution started to admit 'private patients', or women and girls whose time in Bessborough was not funded by the local authorities. The children of women and girls admitted privately were often placed 'at nurse', in a private fostering arrangement, which was often quicker to organise than a 'boarding out' arrangement. Bessborough was often overcrowded and, by the mid-1930s, the Sisters of the Sacred Hearts of Jesus and Mary were running two other institutions, Sean Ross Abbey in Roscrea, County Tipperary, and Castlepollard in County Westmeath.

From the 1940s, the annual reports of government inspectors such as Alice Litster give us a deeper insight into life on the Bessborough estate. Miss Litster describes the 'dark and gloomy' refectory, the potatoes, cheese, cabbage, scallions, rhubarb and tea that she observed at mealtimes and a 'comfortable' recreation room with a pianola. Overall, her surviving reports do not paint an optimistic picture of conditions for women, girls and their children. She repeatedly pointed out poor record-keeping, which, she said, 'bore little relation to the facts'; overcrowding; low rates of breastfeeding; and a lack of contact between mothers and babies, something that would continue well into Joan's time in the home. The matron of the maternity hospital was, in Litster's view, a 'hard person', who did not have any professional nursing qualifications. In addition, Litster criticised local authorities for the delays in placing children with foster families, with some children remaining in the institution over the age of six.[3] The pieces of her reports I could access do not quote the women, girls and children directly so it is impossible to include their views of the institution at that time.

The most distressing details were her descriptions of the health of the younger children. In 1943, she observed that their condition gave 'cause for uneasiness', describing them, in a heartbreaking sentence, as 'miserable scraps of humanity, wizened, some emaciated and almost all had rash and sores all over their bodies, faces, hands and heads'. Death rates soared in Bessborough in the 1940s and, in 1943, 75 per cent of infants born there died. Looking through the list of names of the children who died that year, I could see that the youngest child, Mary Ryan, described as 'daughter of maid', lived for only fifteen minutes and died of a 'premature birth'.[4] The deaths were not always certified by a doctor and often the recorded cause was non-specific – for example, marasmus, a form of malnutrition.

Though Alice Litster recommended that the home be closed to new admissions for at least three months in 1944, this was not acted upon by government or local officials and the congregation of the Sisters of the Sacred Hearts of Jesus and Mary. Meanwhile the deaths continued. A few months later, Bessborough was again inspected, this time by Ireland's chief medical officer, Dr James Deeny. In his 1989 memoir *To Cure and to Care*, Dr Deeny said he 'took a notion and stripped all the babies', examining them. His instincts proved to be correct. 'Every baby had some purulent infection of the skin and all had green diarrhoea, carefully covered up ... The deaths had been going on for years. They [the matron and medical officer] had done nothing about it, had accepted the situation and were quite complacent about it.'

Eventually, Bessborough was closed to women and girls maintained by local authorities in 1945, though those who could pay privately continued to be admitted during that time. Efforts to appoint a replacement matron were delayed by the bishop of Cork, who argued that the government had no right to interfere with a religious appointment. A new matron took over later that year and a medical officer was recruited as well as additional nursing staff. Admissions resumed in 1946, and from the late forties, the death rate started to decrease, though it did rise again to 10 per cent between 1958 and 1960. Improved sanitary facilities and advancements in medical science likely contributed to lowering the death rate, but it is clear that without the intervention of Alice Litster many more children would likely have died in Bessborough.

The high rate of deaths haunted Joan, and in our interviews she often talked about women she had met whose children had died in Bessborough. 'It didn't matter what went on inside the home ... it didn't matter whether your baby died,' she told me. But she was also aware that the children who did survive and left Bessborough were not always well treated. Looking through inspection reports, I could see that foster families and local authorities often failed to put the needs of children first. 'Too often the maintenance allowance, which will add to the family resources, is the main reason for application, or an older child is required who will help to look after the younger members of the family,' wrote Alice Litster in 1931. While some foster homes provided a stable environment for children, it was deeply disturbing to discover that in others children were neglected, beaten and sometimes forced to do child labour on farms.

A small number of children born in Bessborough were not fostered or placed 'at nurse' but were transferred to other institutions, like industrial schools. Others were informally adopted in Ireland, before it became legal in the early 1950s, or were placed for adoption with families in the United States, Great Britain, Canada and Northern Ireland.[5] It was very rare that children left with their mothers or other family members. In the early and middle decades at least, the fate of most surviving children born in the Bessborough institution was to be separated from their natural mothers.

In 1967, the year Joan was admitted to Bessborough, many aspects of the way the institution was run remained unchanged from earlier decades. The system of house names persisted, as did the emphasis on religious redemption and penance. She described it as 'like a prison ... [we were told] we did evil work and we would never make anything of our lives'. But unlike in the twenties, thirties and forties, women and girls in the fifties and sixties spent shorter periods of time in the home. The main reason for this was the introduction of legislation making adoption legal in Ireland, which came into effect on 1 January 1953. The adoptions were carried out under a closed system, where there was no contact or sharing of information between the adopted child and the natural parents. People who wanted to adopt had to be deemed 'of good moral character' and with 'sufficient means to support the child' but it was left up to individual adoption agencies to determine how they would assess this.[6] Examining the text of the law, which required the consent of the mother or guardian, I thought of Joan's account of the day David was taken from her. 'She snatched my son out of my hands ... they just took him,' she told me.

Reading about mixed-race children born in mother and baby institutions, I was reminded of Joan's descriptions of Mary and her son Liam. The children were generally the sons and daughters of Irish women and international students, many from African countries, who had come to study in Ireland under Irish government schemes run to support those newly independent states. Officials expressed concern over whether it would be possible to find adoptive families for the children. A letter from the Adoption Board to the Sacred Heart

Adoption Society at Bessborough stated: 'As the couple live in an isolated rural area, the Board expressed reservations about the desirability of placing a mixed-race child with them.'[7] Similar concerns were expressed about children with disabilities and their disabilities sometimes prevented or delayed adoption. A doctor who examined a child born in Bessborough in the 1960s described them as having a 'low mentality', adding 'It is unlikely that this child will ever be fit for adoption.' The records of St Anne's Adoption Society, which worked closely with Bessborough, described some children as 'unadoptable'.[8]

Other unsettling aspects of life in Bessborough are alluded to in the dry, scientific language of medical journals. 'We are indebted to the medical officers in charge of the children's homes ... for permission to carry out this investigation on infants under their care,' wrote the authors of a study in the *British Medical Journal* in 1962.[9] The article referred to a trial for a Wellcome Laboratories four-in-one vaccine for diphtheria, whooping cough, tetanus and polio. It began in December 1960 and twenty-five children from Bessborough were selected for the study. The authors did not mention that consent was not sought from the mothers or guardians of the children, breaching the ethical standards of the time. It is likely that another trial was undertaken – at least partially – in Bessborough in 1964, this time to test a Glaxo Laboratories measles vaccine.[10] If Joan's son David had been born a couple of years earlier, he might have been selected for a Glaxo

Laboratories five-in-one vaccine trial carried out on sixteen infants in the institution in 1965. Or if he had been born a year later, he might have been part of an experimental infant milk trial that was conducted in the home in 1968 and 1969, also on behalf of Glaxo Laboratories.[11]

By the late 1960s, the number of women and girls confined in Bessborough had increased steadily, reaching its peak in the early 1970s. Thousands like Joan passed through the home: young women and girls who had no access to contraception and whose limited knowledge of sex was gleaned from the agony aunt pages in magazines or conversations with friends. Perhaps, like Joan, they had never heard of institutions like Bessborough and, like her, they spent their first night there wondering when someone was going to collect them and take them home.

After she left Bessborough, Joan was sent to her aunt's house in Portsmouth, where she looked after her three young cousins while thinking about the son she had left behind; she walked along the beach and tried to make herself small. She felt judged by her aunt, who, she said, called her a 'disgrace' and told her she was lucky to be taken in. After a few months, she moved to London and trained as a nurse. Though still a teenager, her youthful innocence was gone, and at night she wondered if her baby too was lost forever.

Chapter Eight

LONDON, 1974

'Is this your first child?' the woman in the next bed asked her.

Baby Julie* stretched out her tiny arms. She had wisps of dark hair and delicate ears and ankles and Joan couldn't tear her eyes away from the small bundle who belonged to her, yawning and about to stir.

'Yes, yes it is.'

'What a little princess.'

Joan smiled as the other woman turned over on her side. Here in London, no one had to know. And the staff had understood. With her five years of nursing experience she knew it was important to tell the midwives about her first baby. 'I don't want this to be disclosed,' she'd told them, and they'd nodded. It was just easier not to talk about it, avoid any mention of it. Seven years had passed since she'd had David and Joan tried her hardest never to think about it all.

Eamonn* will be so thrilled, she thought. He would come in later after work on the building sites, delighted with their new little family. They'd met at a dancehall in Hammersmith and had got married three years ago, a knees-up over a pub in a borrowed dress. She hadn't dared to mention her time in Bessborough at first, but once he started dropping hints outside jewellery shops she knew she'd have to tell him about David. 'It's fine with me as long as my friends and family don't find out about it,' he had said then. And Joan felt the muscles in her chest relax and the plan for the wedding had gone ahead. She hadn't mentioned it again since then, and Eamonn never asked.

They were very different, she and Eamonn, but they muddled along together. He had grown up with lots of siblings crammed into a tiny west of Ireland cottage and had got a job on the buildings as soon as he was old enough. To Joan, Eamonn was decent, he worked hard, he accepted her as she was. And another man wouldn't be as tolerant as Eamonn, of that much she was certain. Other women like her never married, never had other children, never got a second chance. She'd seen for herself how some of them had stayed in Bessborough until their skin creased around their mouths and their hair silvered at the temples.

The midwife returned on her rounds, stopping to look in at the babies and to answer questions from the new mothers on the ward. At the end of Joan's bed, she cooed at Julie.

'How soon should I start getting her into a routine?' Joan asked.

The midwife laughed. 'Relax, Joan, you know all about this, it's your second one.'

Joan said nothing, keeping her eyes on Julie as the midwife continued along the ward.

'I thought you said it was your first one?' she heard from the next bed.

'She is, she is. The midwife's got me mixed up with somebody else.'

Joan willed her cheeks not to burn, to turn away from the memory of the days after David had been born. Not now, she told herself. Eamonn would be there soon, she'd go home to the house they had bought together, to fill it with photos and toys and games. Maybe one day, when Julie was old enough to understand, she'd let her know that she had a brother, but for the moment she couldn't let her mind dwell on the past; she couldn't let anything distract her.

Chapter Nine

LONDON, 1980

Joan picked up her bag and reached for her coat. The leftover turkey and ham were in the fridge, all Eamonn had to do was heat them up, and the children, Julie and Emmett*, six and three, were still excited by their Christmas toys and the tree in the sitting room.

'Bye, Eamonn,' she called. She'd told him she had some shopping to do, that she wanted to take advantage of the sales, maybe get some new clothes for the kids. He hadn't batted an eyelid – she made the same trip the day after Boxing Day every year. She closed the door of the little house they'd scrimped and saved to buy as newlyweds and got into the car. It would be easier on the Tube, but the cramped space made her feel hemmed in, so she avoided it as much as she could.

Music blared in the department store, Christmas hits already starting to feel a bit tired. It was already packed but she never minded the bustle, the people elbowing each other out of the way for a bargain. It had become part of the ritual of this day, this time she allowed herself to remember David. Today was his birthday. He would be thirteen today, a teenager, ten years older than Emmett, her youngest son. Did he get a nice Christmas gift? she wondered. An album, or a Swatch watch, or a football? Did he look like the boys his age she had seen in Ireland when she'd gone back for a summer visit, dragging hurls along the ground, sliotars weighing down their pockets?

A familiar tightness formed in her chest. Over the years, she had become very good at making the best of things, at tucking away any inconvenient thoughts. And there were lots of things to distract her, a thirty-two-year-old woman with two children, a life full of bedtime stories and loud games and sticky little hands in hers. She tried so hard to sort everything into neat compartments in her mind: the work box, the family box, the box for her feelings about the child she left behind in Ireland. The trick, she'd come to learn, was never to let things get mixed up, never to let any thoughts of her previous life spill over into life at home.

She picked up a boy's jumper off the rack. The fashion was all bright colours these days – she wondered if his hair had darkened, whether bold colours would suit him. Would he prefer a football shirt? What team did he support? She watched the other shoppers as they grabbed the bargains and hurried over to the checkout. She envied them, the confidence they had in what they were buying, when she had no idea what her own son would like. One day I'll know what to get him, she told herself. I'll look for him and I'll give him a present he'll love. The kids aren't old enough yet, but as soon as they are, I'll tell them everything too.

But that was enough for now. It was time to seal off the box, go back to the kids and join in their games, eat what was left of the Christmas chocolates. She hung the jumper back on the rail and walked away from the crowd.

Chapter Ten

LONDON, 1987

Joan collected the dinner plates and brought them into the kitchen. I'm going to do it today, she thought. No more putting it off. At thirteen and ten, Julie and Emmett would be well able to grasp what she was about to say to them. She'd keep it short. Just a couple of sentences with the bare facts and she'd answer their questions honestly. Still, the thought of it made her feel nervous. There were no manuals for things like this. How do you break it to your children that they have a brother they never knew about?

She set down the plates in the sink. The last of the evening light was coming in the kitchen window of her west London home. She'd started to think the house was too big for them. It was a friendly neighbourhood alright, full of aspirational families like themselves, Irish and South Asian, and the houses were well-kept semi-detached Victorians with spacious gardens and ample-sized rooms. But she'd preferred their previous house, a three-up, two-down, with its small galley kitchen. It had been cosier, easier to manage. Between the children and her shifts as a night sister on a surgical ward, keeping on top of everything felt like a daily marathon.

Turning off the TV, she cleared her throat.

'I've got something to tell you.'

'What is it, Mum?' asked Julie, a slight annoyance on her face that her programme had been interrupted.

'I've thought about it for a long time and I think you're old enough to know now,' Joan continued. 'Your father knows about it, and I don't want to keep it a secret from you.'

Julie and Emmett nodded, their eyes fixed on her.

'You have another brother. He was born in 1967 so he'd be a grown-up young man now, probably finished school already. I had him when I was very young. I couldn't keep him so he lives with another family in Ireland.'

She glanced at them, waiting to register the shock on their faces. But their expressions had barely changed.

'I love him very much but it just wasn't possible to have him with me.'

'OK,' said Julie in a measured tone. 'Thanks for telling us, Mum.'

Emmett, normally full of chat and mischief, stayed silent.

Joan turned the TV back on and went back to the dishes

in the kitchen, deflated. What else could she have expected? They were still only kids, after all. And what if they'd wanted to know what he looked like? She didn't even have a photograph to show them.

She heard the key turn in the lock. Eamonn always got back late, working long days on the sites.

'Hi, Joan,' he said, hanging up his coat and washing his hands in the sink. His hair was streaked with grey and his hands gnarled from the sites but he was still a handsome man. If she was honest with herself, she'd stopped expecting too much from the marriage. Eamonn had his good points. He was kind to her and the children, a hard worker and a great provider. But he was never the type to do the washing or change the nappies or even take the kids to the park. And she wasn't unhappy; she loved the birthday parties and school events and the GAA matches for her London-Irish children with English accents. But deep down, even with her nursing friends and her job, Joan couldn't shake the feeling that something was not quite right, that she wasn't quite where she was supposed to be. If she found herself with a moment to daydream, she imagined herself doing the ward round in an Irish hospital, settling in a town where she knew her neighbours, sending the children to a local school where they'd learn Irish, and savouring a slower pace of life. But Eamonn had never been keen; he had left his tiny village with no desire to ever go back – home to him was London now, their house, their kitchen table, their little patch of lawn. As the children got older and started primary school, Joan told herself it would be a few more years, then when Julie started secondary, she realised that her imagination was just running away with her; it wasn't as if they could pack up and leave, just like that.

'I told Julie and Emmett about David,' she said, setting down his dinner in the dining room.

'Oh. How was it?'

'They seemed to accept it. They haven't asked any questions.'

'Great. Good that they know that now,' he said, returning to his plate.

Joan looked at the clock: it was time to get ready for the next night shift. Objectively, it had gone well with the kids. But it would be nice to have a proper conversation about her other son occasionally. Even her closest friends in London didn't know about him. But what would she tell them? That her son was taken from her by nuns in a creaky Georgian house she spent hours cleaning? That she hadn't signed any papers? That her mother and stepfather had decided that placing David for adoption was the best thing to do and that Joan had thought there was nothing she could do to stop it? Joan feared seeing a grain of doubt in their eyes as they listened, and that would be the worst thing of all.

Upstairs, Joan got her things together in her bag, checked

she had her purse and her badge. Even all these years later, it still amazed her how a career she had chosen only to get away from her aunt's house in Portsmouth could have brought her so much fulfilment. There were always cards and boxes of chocolates around the house from patients or their families and Joan kept them as a reminder that she was someone who contributed positively to the world. 'They'll think I can't afford to keep you,' Eamonn had joked when she'd decided to go back to work after the children were born, but she'd ignored him. She'd switched to district nursing for the first few years and, now that the kids were a bit older, she'd gone back to the hospital, where she was quickly promoted to night sister.

It was in the hospital that she'd had the only meaningful conversation about her past. It had been a couple of years back and she and an agency nurse called Liz were enjoying a rare quiet moment in her office. Joan had got on well with Liz, an Irish woman in her forties with dark, curly hair and a ready smile and a capable member of Joan's team. She could still remember the look of seriousness on her face.

'If I'm wrong about this, and God forgive me if I am, or if what I'm about to say upsets you, just tell me,' Liz had said. 'Did you have a baby in Bessborough?'

Joan had paused, taking a deep breath. 'Yes, I did,' she'd replied, exhaling deeply. It felt good to admit it to someone else, to get the words out.

'I thought it was you. I was in there at the same time as

you. I recognised your voice – you still haven't lost the Cork accent. Do you remember me? My house name was Ann.'

It had taken Joan a second to place Liz, but then she'd remembered Ann, the girl who'd bathed her just after David was born. Her voice had the same kind timbre, slightly huskier now with age, but it was unmistakable.

'You were so kind to me then. I never got a chance to thank you.'

Liz had nodded, smiling. 'You must have left long before me because I don't remember seeing you after that. I stayed in that godforsaken place until my son was one and a half – he wasn't adopted because he had a slight deformity in his left hand. The nuns started encouraging me to go. They found me a cleaning job in Dún Laoghaire, and I could take my son. It was a start but when I got there I had to leave him on his own in the room sometimes to get the work done and I hated that. When I had enough money saved, I got on the ferry with him and came here. It was hard, but I got work, and I got married and had other children, two lovely girls. And I trained as a nurse. I love it. And to be honest I'm glad I have a career because the marriage broke up and we're separated now. My son – Jim is his name – he has an English accent now; he works in a carpet shop, not far from here.'

And as the machines had beeped and a hush had fallen on the ward, Joan had told her how she'd left Bessborough just two days after David was taken from her; how she'd sat on the next flight to London in her crumpled clothes; how after a few months she'd applied to nursing school because she would have done anything, literally anything, to get out of her aunt's house. And as Liz had listened, Joan had told her that for the first few years, she'd almost blocked Bessborough from her mind, the years whizzing by as she'd got her nursing qualification and married Eamonn and moved into their first little house. But then she'd had Julie and Emmett and she'd realised all she'd missed out on, the wobbly steps and the first kicks of a football, all the things she'd never be around to see. Liz had listened as Joan had told her that she'd been at the airport that summer, going back home to visit her brother, and she'd scanned all the young men she saw there, in case one of them might be David. And then she'd tried to snap out of it because it wouldn't do her any good but she'd wished more than anything that she could know that he was happy. And Liz had nodded, her eyes full of compassion, as Joan had told her she wanted to search for him one day, but not yet, she wasn't ready yet.

Then the moment was over; it was time to get back to the patients. Sometimes, as she made her journey to work, to do those same rounds, Joan thought of that conversation with Liz. She'd since moved onto another agency job but Joan wondered how many other Bessborough girls she'd come across in London, how many more, like her, with good jobs and good lives, kept the same secrets.

Chapter Eleven

LONDON, 1989

Joan felt the basket of shopping drop from her hand before it fell with a thud by the cash register. The tomatoes scattered across the floor; the carrots and the potatoes started to roll under the nearby shelves. But she couldn't stop to pick them up. Her heart had started to pound in her chest, and the supermarket ceiling, with its fluorescent lights, spun above her head. She felt dizzy, her breathing obstructed by an invisible weight pressing down on her chest. I have to get out, she thought.

Julie and Emmett looked at her, their faces red with embarrassment.

'Are you OK, Mum?'

Joan gestured towards the door; she couldn't get the words out. I have to get out, she wanted to shout.

'Mum, are you sure you're alright?'

In the car, she had to take a second before she could get the keys into the ignition.

'It's alright, I'll settle in a second and we'll head home,' she told them.

Her hands shook as she gripped the steering wheel and put the car into gear.

At home, when Julie and Emmett were in bed, she sat at the kitchen table and reflected on what had happened, the panic that had paralysed her. She had thought that the shop ceiling was about to fall down on top of her, and that she would be trapped under a pile of dust and rubble. There were other things, too, that bothered her. There was her trouble with lifts; she couldn't bear the feeling of being enclosed. And Eamonn and the kids had noticed that she always wanted to leave the windows open. She'd had to ask one of the doctors in the hospital for some strategies to manage things. 'Have you ever suffered a trauma?' he'd asked her then. And Joan had said she hadn't, had pushed all thoughts of Bessborough's tiny 'cell' out of her mind. There was nothing in her past that could explain it, she told him, nothing at all.

Chapter Twelve

DONEGAL, 2001

Joan flicked the switch on the kettle and looked out the window. A watery sun broke through the clouds and lit up the garden of the small B&B she was running since she'd moved back to Ireland. She never tired of the stark, bleakly beautiful landscapes of a Donegal holiday town: grey mostly, but glimpses of blues and yellows and purples when the fog lifted. All that space made her heart feel light, and with every day that passed she grew more confident in her decision to take early retirement. She'd loved being a nurse, and then a social worker when she'd retrained in her early forties, but as she'd entered her fifties and the children had finished university, she had felt it was time for a change.

She lived alone, but with guests coming and going, she never felt lonely. And if she was really honest with herself, she enjoyed her own company; over the years she and Eamonn had come to an agreement that they were better off not living together, that they'd put the children first. They'd divorced, amicably, a few years ago; Joan had recognised that they were too different. And, secretly, she hoped being back in Ireland would help bring her closer to finding David. It was the next thing on her list now that she was settled in.

She sat down with a cup of tea, grateful for a few moments of calm before she started the routine of sheet ironing, jam making and egg collecting that occupied her days. In the newspaper she'd bought that morning, there were more reports about the foot and mouth disease outbreaks, the animal culls in the UK and Ireland. Scanning the page, she read an article further down. Then she sat up straight in her chair with a jolt.

She looked at the paper again, checking that she had indeed got it right. She had. There it was, in small black letters at the bottom of a news article: a helpline number for people who had spent time in Ireland's institutions as children. She noted it down carefully in her notepad and picked up the receiver. Her heart raced. As far as she knew, David had been adopted, not sent to an institution, but surely the people at the other end of the line would be able to point her in the right direction?

After a couple of rings, she got through to a man called Tadhg. His voice was kind, she thought. She took a second to gather herself. It was hard to admit these things to a stranger, but at least she didn't have to do it face to face.

'I had a baby boy in the Bessborough mother and baby institution in 1967. I'm looking to trace him.'

'Bessborough. I see. That's a bit tricky for us, Joan, because we don't deal with mother and baby institutions or with tracing. Do you know if he got sent anywhere else afterwards? Did they tell you he was being transferred to an institution?'

Joan's cheeks burned. 'No, nothing. I don't know anything at all.'

There was a pause; Joan could tell Tadhg was choosing his next words carefully.

'You're not the first person to call us looking for information. We get about eight phone calls a week from women who were in mother and baby institutions. It's hard to know where to start. Do you have any records?'

'No, nothing. I don't have anything from my time there.'

'Listen, Joan, I'm really sorry to say this, but your son might even be in America. A lot of children were adopted by American families at that time. There are some groups around that might be able to give you a bit more information, but unfortunately there's nothing I can do for you here.'

Joan felt every ounce of the optimism of the morning ebb away. Could David really be in the States? He'd be thirty-four now, maybe married with a family of his own. Did he live in Idaho, New York or San Francisco? And with no records of any kind, how could she even begin to trace him?

❖

A few weeks later, she found a number for the Sacred Heart Adoption Society, Bessborough, and as she dialled it she could feel a surge of adrenaline rushing through her veins. She got through to a Sister Philomena, explained that she wanted to search for her son.

'I see. I came here in the early 1970s so I wouldn't have been there during your time.'

Something in her tone made Joan tense with anger, but she tried to keep her voice light. 'I'd like to arrange to come down to Bessborough and collect my files.'

'I see. We'll have to get back to you on that, Joan.'

Joan felt a rage bubbling up inside her. Why this attitude? In the UK they'd been reuniting people without fuss for years. 'I want to make sure that the congregation are held accountable for what they did, for treating people so cruelly, for taking children away from their mothers without their permission. I have spent almost thirty-five years wishing that my son was with me, worrying about where he was, whether he was OK, whether he was loved and cared for.'

'I can tell that you're angry, Joan. A lot of women like you ring up. What I can offer you is a reconciliation service, and I think it would be to your benefit. The next time you're in Cork, do ring me up, and we'll meet for reconciliation.'

Joan slammed the phone down. Reconciliation? Not a chance, she thought. Why was a system not in place to help her trace her son? Even the tiniest scrap of information would stop her mind from wandering.

Chapter Thirteen

CORK, 2011

The robins scrabbled around Joan's birdfeeder, picking at the nuts and plump seeds through the wire mesh. Her sweet pea was long gone, the weather just starting to get cooler, the first of the autumn leaves crunching underfoot. It had a different feel, Cork, to Donegal, but even after six years back in her home county she still felt a deep peace whenever she looked out the patio door of her one-bedroom flat. She didn't miss it, the B&B. Now fully retired, she had swapped hosting guests for long walks by the sea with her daughter Julie – who had moved back to Ireland to be near Joan – and Julie's two children, Neil* and Ava*. For the first time in years, Joan lived in a place that felt like a home.

Her mobile beeped. A text from Julie. 'Anything yet?'

Joan texted back a quick response. 'No, nothing.'

It had been stop-start, stop-start for the past few years, Julie supporting her through every step of her search to find David. They'd trawled through genealogy websites in the US, coming up against dead end after dead end. And, together, they had phoned and written to every adoption society they could think of for advice on how to proceed. Every time, the answer was the same. 'We have no records for you on file,' a voice on the other end of the line would tell Joan. Because she hadn't signed any papers or been told anything at the time, she had no information of any kind to help refine the search. She hadn't contacted Bessborough again after her encounter with Sister Philomena, but just a few weeks earlier, she'd sent a letter to her local TD about access to adoption files from the institution.

Stepping into her kitchen-cum-dining-room, she put the phone back on her table. I've spent ten years searching for him, she thought, the muscles around her temples tightening with stress. Why must this be so hard?

❖

A few weeks later, a letter arrived in the post in response to her questions. Joan read it twice. There was a phone number. There was an address. There was a process. This was progress. The letter read:

A system has been put in place to manage queries from clients, i.e. children born in the Sacred Heart Homes (now adults) and birth mothers ... The HSE has already commenced responding to individual queries and encourages anyone seeking their personal data to communicate directly with the HSE South Adoption Unit, St Stephen's Hospital, Glanmire, County Cork.

On paper, at least, it was simple. All Joan had to do was follow the instructions and someone would help her to find out more information. She grabbed her keys and got in her car. She was done with letters and emails.

The social worker on duty in the unit was curt.

'There is a process,' she explained. 'I can't just hand you over the records.'

'Just tell me what it is.'

The social worker responded crisply. 'You have to write a letter. Then we put you on a waiting list. You have to bear with us.'

'I've been patient for the last forty-four years. All I'm asking you is: is my file there?'

'I'm sorry, Joan, that's all I can do for you for the moment.'

Joan made her way back to the car. Yet another letter, she thought. She wondered if all the paper would leave a trail that her son might trace back to her or if it would end up stuffing a dusty folder in a filing cabinet.

❖

Joan wrote the letter. The response was short and matter of fact:

> *As you appreciate we have received a substantial amount of requests for a service, we are presently organising these enquiries in date order. Once we have assessed the nature of each request, we will contact you as soon as possible. We appreciate your patience.*

Joan, incensed, picked up the phone. Did people actually understand what had gone on, she wondered, what it was like to not know where your child was, how, even now, she still felt shame corroding her insides?

'I'm in my sixties. I could be dead in a few years. My information is out there somewhere. Someone must have it.'

'I'm sorry, Joan, but we can't give you any more information at the moment. We'll be in touch.'

Why all the bloody bureaucracy? she thought as she slammed down the phone. Guidelines, policies and procedures were necessary, but Ireland was light years behind the UK. Things didn't need to be so difficult.

Chapter Fourteen

CORK, 2013

Joan turned the key in the lock and dashed into her flat. Dropping her gym bag in the hall, she flopped onto the couch and gave a satisfied sigh. Twice a week she put herself through a set routine: weights and cardio for strength and endurance. And the exercise-induced high she felt now gave her a confidence boost for what she was about to do.

She picked up her mobile, dialling the number for the social worker assigned to her case.

'Any update?'

'Not since the last time you phoned me. Joan, you have to be patient. I'll get back to you as soon as I can. These things take time.' Joan could hear the hint of exasperation in her voice. For the past six months, Joan had been phoning her every week.

She put down the phone. None of this makes any sense, she thought. There was no way of knowing how things were progressing. She had to stop herself from thinking about things too deeply, about how the years were passing her by and she still hadn't got any closer to finding her son.

In January, her mobile rang.

'Joan, I have good news for you. We've found your file,' the social worker told her.

'About bloody time.' The words were out of her mouth before she'd even had a chance to consider them.

'We have located your son and he has told us that he wants to make contact with you. He's been searching for you for the past nine years.' Then the social worker told her about lost files and papers falling out of a drawer but Joan didn't really take it all in. Her son was alive, she finally knew that for certain. He was living in Ireland, not America. And after all these years, he wanted to meet her. She'd get to see him, be in the same room as him, hear his voice.

The rest of the day passed in a haze, Joan almost drunk on the good news, and only when it had fully sunk in did she remember the other part of the phone call. Her son had been trying to meet her for nearly a decade, perhaps writing the same letters and emails and making the same phone calls that she had. The delays had kept them apart. All that lost time, and she could never get it back. But she couldn't focus on that now, not after how far she'd come.

A few weeks later, she got another letter, followed by a phone call from the social worker to say that her son had written to them with a note for her. She read it over and over again after it arrived, studying the tone and the language used, for any clues as to what her son might be like. It was short, to the point, and warm. Her son was living in Ireland, was a farmer in the midlands, his adoptive name was Walter* and he was married. He wanted to meet her, he couldn't wait, he said, and he'd tell her all about himself then. There were a couple of photographs: he was a strongly built fair-haired man with a warm smile; around the eyes he looked like her daughter Julie. Joan scanned every inch of the photo; each time she looked at it, she could see the trace of a relative in him.

That evening, she tore out pages and pages of foolscap, drafting and redrafting her own lines until she could find the right combination, failed attempts littering the kitchen floor. Even when she'd finished, she still wasn't quite sure she'd got it right. How much enthusiasm was appropriate? How much was too little?

'Only photographs of yourself at this stage,' the social worker had told her. But Joan couldn't help herself. She put in photos of herself, the dog, Julie and Emmett – who were fully supportive of her search – and her grandchildren.

When she was finished, she picked up the phone again to the social worker. 'We want to meet each other – we stated that in the letters we wrote. When is it going to happen?'

'We have to wait, we have to ensure that ... that it's right for you.'

'Set a date. I'm not putting up with it any more. Set a date.'

The poor woman, Joan sometimes thought, she was just doing her job. But the whole system was so inefficient it infuriated her.

Regional Adoption Service
Child and Family Agency
Páirc na gCrann
St Stephen's Hospital
Sarsfield Court
County Cork
15 April 2014
Our ref: _____
Private and Confidential

Dear Joan,
I am enclosing the card from Walter and a lovely selection of photos that he wishes you to have. I am very happy for you and Walter that you have this opportunity to have contact with each other. Having discussed the matter with you and Walter, I am aware that you are both happy to proceed to a reunion

in the near future. As discussed during our phone calls, I am therefore happy to set a provisional date for your reunion.

Date: Wednesday, 7th May 2014
Venue: Adoption Department, St Stephen's Hospital, Sarsfield Court, Glanmire.

I will contact you closer to this date to finalise details for your reunion with Walter.
I wish you and all your family a Happy Easter.
Kind regards,

_____

SOCIAL WORKER

Chapter Fifteen

CORK, 2014

Joan stood in front of the mirror, brushing her hair for a second time. She looked rather well, she thought, considering she hadn't slept very well the night before. She had chosen the navy trouser suit – she always wore it when she wanted to look smart but not too formal. He wanted to meet her one time at least, she told herself. That was a positive step. If that's as far as it goes, it's better than nothing, she reasoned. But there was one doubt that was trickier to put out of her mind. Would he understand? she wondered.

Her hands trembled as she turned the keys in the ignition. What would she say to him? Would it be awkward? Would she shake his hand or give him a hug? She pulled up at the adoption department's offices in Glanmire just before eleven, outside an uninviting 1960s building behind the flat-roofed St Stephen's Hospital. As she parked, she could see Walter standing in the car park, a huge smile on his face, next to the social worker. When she opened the car door and got out, he swooped her up in the air.

The social worker's face fell. 'You've done it all wrong,' she told them. 'Come inside'.

Joan wondered what the right way would have been.

The social worker ushered them into a tiny room with small chairs, soft toys and dolls. Was it used to interview children? Joan wondered. She glanced at Walter; he looked awkward, perching his big frame on a plastic chair. The relaxed moment in the car park had disappeared, replaced by an atmosphere that felt slightly tense.

'Did it take long for you to get down this morning? What time did you leave?' Joan asked. As soon as the words were out of her mouth, she regretted them. They sounded banal, like idle chit-chat. She looked around; the social worker was taking notes and it made her feel even more uncomfortable. She had the urge to cough, one of her occasional coughing fits left over from a winter cold, and then she found she wasn't able to gather herself. Walter and the social worker looked up at her, waiting for the coughs to die down, but she couldn't stop.

The social worker stepped in. 'Do you want a glass of water?'

'Yes please,' Joan replied, struggling in between coughs.

Once the social worker had left the room, Walter turned to her.

'Listen, it's a bit formal in here. Do you want to go for lunch somewhere else?'

Joan knew instantly that she wanted to say yes. 'I'd love that,' she said, barely getting the words out.

Walter smiled and Joan felt herself relax. Thank God for that, she thought. By the time the social worker came back in, Joan had collected herself once again. She and Walter stood up, ready to leave.

'It's OK, we're going to lunch,' Joan told the social worker.

'Please just stay until we've finished the session.'

'No, absolutely not, we've got to go.'

In a nearby hotel, the conversation flowed more naturally. Joan could barely take her eyes off Walter. This was the tiny baby who had been taken away, now well over six feet tall, a man in his late forties. It was difficult to adjust to it.

'I never stopped thinking about you,' she told him. 'Never. If I was out somewhere and I saw somebody around the same age as you that I thought looked a bit like me, I used to think to myself: Would that be my son? Every single year on your birthday, I remembered you.'

'I used to imagine what you were like all the time too,' he said. 'When I was a teenager, I used to think: My mother is out there somewhere, and I know she's going to go looking for me. I just knew you'd find me.'

When they asked for the bill, Joan wasn't ready for the meeting to end so soon. Walter had had a lot of questions and she'd had such a good time telling him about Julie and Emmett.

'I don't live too far from Julie. Would you like to meet her? I could text her and she could meet us at my flat.'

'I'd love that.' And Joan knew he meant it – there hadn't been a second's hesitation.

Inside the flat, she gestured for him to make himself comfortable on the couch.

'Do you take sugar?'

He nodded. It felt odd, having to ask the question. She knew down to the precise measurements how many sweeteners Julie took and what kind of biscuits Emmett liked.

They had a few quiet moments with their tea before Julie burst in. 'You're the reason I've been demoted from the eldest to the middle child,' she told Walter, 'so I expect you'll make that up to me.'

Walter laughed and Joan felt any worries she had melt away. The conversation flowed into the evening and Julie's children, Neil and Ava, came over to meet their new family member.

'Hi, Uncle Walter,' they said, getting involved in the jokes and the family stories being shared.

That night, after she bid everyone goodbye and cleared the dishes, Joan collapsed in an exhausted heap. I can stop wondering now, she thought. After forty-six years, I've found him.

A couple of weeks later, Joan checked she had everything in her handbag. She was on the early-morning train from Cork to Dublin, to meet Walter on Werburgh Street, outside the General Register Office. They were on a shared mission – to access Walter's birth certificate, because he only had an adoption certificate. Previously, when he had applied to Túsla, the Child and Family Agency, for information, he had been given Joan's first name only. Without a surname, he didn't have enough detail to enable him to search for his birth certificate.

On the street she saw him approach, and she felt a rush of fondness for him, this big bulky farmer who was her son.

'Hi, Walter,' she said, smiling. It was still tricky to get used to calling him by his adoptive name.

He smiled back and she felt more at ease.

Inside, Joan gave him all the details he needed. His information was located in the registers within minutes. When they paid the fee and got a photocopy, Walter stared at it for a couple of minutes, visibly moved.

'You know, so many times, when I filled out paperwork for the cattle to comply with EU regulations, I wondered why I couldn't access the same details about myself. I remember sitting in the barn and looking at the documents. I could go right back to this calf's mother, grandmother, the lineage, and here was I, and I didn't know the faintest thing about who I was.'

Joan made a mental note to make a collage for him with everything she knew about her family history.

She had it ready for him a few weeks later when they met for lunch at a location halfway between where they both lived. She'd dug out photos of her own grandparents, her mother, her father, of Julie and Emmett, some childhood photos, anything she could find that might help him piece together his knowledge of the people who had existed before him.

'He's a vet,' Walter said when she told him about his grandfather. Joan knew he was joining the dots in his mind, a shared love of animals.

'Tell me about your adoptive family, what it was like for you growing up?' she asked him. 'I'd love to know a bit more.'

'To be honest, things weren't great.'

Joan shifted in her seat, nodding at Walter to continue.

'We didn't have a good relationship. And I never really got many details about why they decided to take me in. I don't really like talking about it.'

Joan felt her stomach twist with guilt. Over the years, she had assumed that couples who adopted children did so because they couldn't have any of their own and really wanted them; it hadn't entered her head that an adopted child wouldn't be loved or cherished like any other child.

'Once my adoptive mother told me that they had made a donation to the congregation of nuns to get me. Another time she told me that she took me in because you didn't want me, that I would have ended up in an orphanage if she hadn't.'

'I always—'

'I know that. I never believed that.'

'In those places, you didn't have any choice, they just did what they wanted.'

'I know that. I understand what went on,' he reassured her.

He doesn't judge me, Joan thought. But later, when she reflected on the raucous birthday parties and the family trips Julie and Emmett had enjoyed, she couldn't stop herself from thinking about all the things she hadn't been able to do for Walter.

Chapter Sixteen

BRUSSELS, 2014

Joan checked the display screen in Dublin Airport and made her way towards the departures terminal. She yawned, thinking about the long journey ahead. She'd driven to Dublin from Cork that morning and shortly she would fly to Brussels. Then there would be the presentation at the European Parliament she'd been preparing for for a couple of weeks now. She'd discussed it with Walter, what she was about to do. She had his full support.

It was the right thing for her, she knew that. For so long, she'd been so focused on trying to find Walter that she hadn't given herself the space to reflect on things. But she'd be sixty-seven soon; she didn't want to live under a fog of shame any longer or siphon a part of herself off from the world. Now, she felt ready to speak out more publicly. In theory, there was nothing to be embarrassed about – none of it had been her fault. But the thought of sharing her experiences with a roomful of strangers made her break into a cold sweat.

Still, she was proud of what she had been able to pull together so quickly. Through a mutual contact, she had got a call from the Sinn Féin MEP Martina Anderson, who had proposed a hearing in the European Parliament to discuss the mother and baby institutions. The issue was high on the news agenda after a local historian, Catherine Corless, had gone public with her research into the deaths of hundreds of children at another mother and baby institution in Tuam. Joan had seized the opportunity, contacting online networks and support groups she had come across over the years. She put together an apolitical delegation of survivors, adopted people and academics to address the European Parliament

Checked in, she headed towards the gate. Mary Linehan-Foley, adopted from Bessborough the year before Walter was born, had travelled with her from Cork. She'd grown up with a lovely family in Youghal and had only recently been reunited with her natural mother. It hadn't been easy, but mother and daughter now got on well. As they waited for the plane and greeted the other members of the delegation, Joan could see Mary asking questions and listening intently to the answers, learning more about a system that had affected her from birth.

❖

Inside the hemicycle building in the Espace Léopold, the flags of the EU member states hung behind the main podium. Camera shutters clicked; journalists sat poised with their laptops. In the crowd she spotted MEPs she recognised from the news. Have I done the right thing? she wondered. The space was huge, and she felt far away from the other speakers sitting at the polished wooden tables. It wasn't that she was shy about public speaking – presentations had been part of her professional life as a social worker. But talking about her own life was so very different.

Looking down at her sheet of paper, Joan cleared her throat.

'In 1967, I gave birth to a son in the Bessborough mother and baby home,' she began, detailing her treatment there, the circumstances of the birth. As she spoke, her voice became clearer and more confident.

'I never agreed to put my son up for adoption, I was never informed about it or given a choice ... In 2000, having spent more than thirty years in exile because of the shame of what I had done, I came back to fight the system and get back my child I did not agree to get rid of ... I still bore the shame of being an unmarried mother so I did all my enquiries in secret and every door was slammed in my face,' she continued.

The auditorium was silent. But Joan felt strangely detached from the experience, as if someone else was speaking.

'I pestered and tormented until I finally got my file. My son was nine years searching for me and encountering the same – they kept us apart when we could have been together.'

By the end of her speech, some in the chamber were in tears. More speakers followed. Rita Tisdall had worked in Temple Hill, a holding centre for children placed for adoption. 'We were not allowed to have physical contact with the babies,' she said. 'They were between a few days old and two years. When they cried we weren't allowed to rock their beds ... You held them on your knee with a hand behind their head and fed them at a distance.' Mary Linehan-Foley's voice shook as she described herself as 'one of the lucky ones', adding that she had learned more about herself in the drive from the airport to the parliament buildings than she had in her whole life up to this point. Susan Lohan of the Adoption Rights Alliance urged politicians to call for a full investigation into the system of adoption in Ireland, in mother and baby homes but also other institutions, such as county homes and maternity hospitals involved in adoptions. 'More than 100,000 women lost their babies,' she said.

Joan felt relieved, lighter somehow, as if someone had removed a breeze block from the top of her chest. She hoped her speech would help others too, like the woman in another part of the country who had contacted her on Facebook a while back. She was still living a life of half-truths; she hadn't told her husband or her children that she had had another child. 'I feel like I deserve this punishment for what I did,' she had told Joan.

It had broken Joan's heart, hearing that.

Chapter Seventeen

PORTLAOISE, 2015

In a conference room in the Heritage Hotel, Joan took a sip of water. She looked around at the small group of women she had connected with via a Facebook group. They all seemed around her own age, maybe a couple were a few years younger. It was their first in-person meeting and, so far, things had been going well. The moderator had stopped speaking and had encouraged a petite woman with short blonde hair to address the group.

'My name is Claire*,' she began. Her voice was a little hesitant and Joan could tell her accent was from the west of Ireland.

'I was in the Bessborough mother and baby institution in 1966,' she continued.

Joan sat up straighter in her seat. She hadn't come across any other women from Bessborough and her friend Liz had died of cancer many years ago in London.

'I was nineteen. I was really red raw from the country. I walked in and I just felt my life was over. The nun told me I would be known as Nellie ... I hated that name. It was so sad. One would start crying and then everyone would be crying. You'd hear the sob, sob, sob from every bed all along the dormitory.'

It sounds just like my own story, Joan thought. And as Claire started to talk about her experience of giving birth in Bessborough, it sounded every bit as harrowing as her own.

'All the nun kept saying was "Stop your shouting" and "What are you shouting for?" I begged her for medicine and she said, "No, you have to pay for your sins."'

Like Joan, Claire's baby boy was taken away from her when he was just a few weeks old.

'In those days, I was afraid to ask questions ... The fear and the loneliness and the sorrow and everything else was just unbearable ... Our lives really were taken from us to an extent ... we spent all our lives wondering where our children were.'

The moderator nodded at Joan, indicating that she too should share her experience.

'I was in Bessborough too, around the same time as Claire,'

she told the group. 'She's explained everything so well already, it's as if she were telling my life story.'

It brought Joan a strange comfort, knowing that someone else remembered things as she remembered them, that her mind hadn't played tricks on her as the years had passed.

After a few months, Claire phoned her. They had connected on Facebook after the meeting, liking and sharing each other's posts and memes, commenting on family photographs. Joan could sense the urgency in her voice.

'Joan, I have some news for you,' she told her. 'My son has got in touch and we've arranged a meeting ... I know you've gone through this process recently so I'm wondering what to expect, if you have any advice for me.'

'That's wonderful, Claire, how did he find you?'

'It was through Facebook. One evening, I couldn't sleep, so I went on the computer to play my word game. I saw a message on Facebook, but not where it would normally be, because it was from someone I wasn't friends with. I clicked on it, and it was from him.'

'I'm so delighted for you.'

'The thing is, he'd sent the message two years ago. I didn't realise until after I told my daughters and they looked at it for me. He had sent it to us on his birthday, two years ago. And I hadn't seen it.'

'So what did you do? Did you reply straight away?'

'No, I was too afraid. My daughter got through to social services and we went to meet a social worker. She said that he had been in touch with them, three years earlier, when he'd changed his address. So I asked if he was in Ireland and she told me he was, but she couldn't give me any information. She said she would contact him and tell him I was looking for him, and that if he wanted to meet me, social services would arrange something. When they wrote to him, he got in touch with me again through Facebook.'

'When are you meeting?'

'He's coming down with his wife at the weekend and they're staying in the hotel near me.'

'And how are you feeling about it?'

'I'm a bit nervous. What if he thinks I'm horrible because I didn't keep him? It's like meeting a total stranger and trying to explain yourself.'

'I think if you can recognise that and not have expectations that are too high, that will help. It's great that he wants to meet you, but at this stage you have no idea where the relationship is going to go. If you manage your expectations, anything that comes with it then will be a bonus, rather than a disappointment. Does that make sense?'

'It does. And my daughter did say to me that he might only want his medical details from my side of the family. So I have to be prepared for that.'

'Good luck, Claire, I'll be thinking of you.'

As she hung up, Joan hoped with all her heart that all would go well. These things were impossible to predict. She'd spoken to another woman who had traced her daughter, but the daughter had told the woman that she didn't want to get to know her and asked her never to contact her again.

Chapter Eighteen

BESSBOROUGH, 2019

Joan hoped the windscreen wipers on her little car would prove sturdy enough to keep up with the rain. The weather was so bad she had wondered earlier that morning if the annual commemoration event at Bessborough would be cancelled. There was a small part of her that had been disappointed when she'd logged on to Facebook to find that it was still on. Would she feel OK afterwards? she wondered.

A sinking feeling formed in her stomach as she drove past the security hut and up the long avenue. You'll be alright, she told herself. It's only for a couple of hours. Parking in front of the house, she took a second to gather herself. The door was still painted a bright red, just as it had been over fifty years before.

As she got out of the car, she noted other things that had been exactly as she had remembered them, the faded grandeur of the house, the well-kept lawns she had tended to all those decades ago. On the steps, she spotted familiar faces milling around, umbrellas being battered in the wind.

She waved at Martha*, a blonde-haired woman adopted from Bessborough she had got to know through a previous commemoration.

Martha smiled. They'd catch up later – the ceremony was about to start.

Joan followed the crowd into a small prefab classroom set up for the occasion to shelter from the rain. It was a pity, really, that the weather was so horrendous: here they'd be bunched in together; it wouldn't be comfortable. Already, the smell of wet coats had started to mix with the aroma of a vat of coffee. Joan got herself a cup of tea and a biscuit, moved to a less crowded corner of the room.

The mood was different this year, Joan could sense it. Just a few weeks earlier, the latest interim report of the Mother and Baby Homes Commission of Investigation, which focused on burial practices in the homes, had come out. Joan had given evidence and was awaiting the final report. The news on burials had shocked everyone in the Bessborough community. Over 900 children had died in Bessborough in the years it had been in operation, or in hospital having been transferred. But the burial places of only sixty-four were known. The commission was also not able to establish where at least fourteen women who died in Bessborough were buried. The congregation of the Sisters of the Sacred Hearts of Jesus and Mary said it did not know where the women and children who died at the home were buried but the commission had said this was 'difficult to comprehend'.

In the classroom, Joan strained to hear the speeches, the crowded room making it difficult for her hearing aids to pick everything up. Fergus Finlay, the head of Barnardos charity for vulnerable children, was the guest speaker. He spoke of the need for each person to be allowed to have a grave, a place where they can be properly remembered, calling for those gathered to press for further action. Carmel Cantwell, a woman in her fifties with curly dark hair and a soft London accent, told the story of her brother William, born in Bessborough in 1960, who died shortly afterwards.

It was a story Joan knew well. Where's Bridget? she wondered, looking around for Carmel and William's mother, before spotting the elegant woman in her late seventies with wide-set blue eyes. She had come to know Bridget over the years. They had met at a previous commemoration and were friends on Facebook, Joan commenting on Bridget's photos of homemade sultana bread or the news articles she shared.

I hope she's alright, Joan thought. She remembered the

first time Bridget told her the story, how vivid Bridget's memories were of her tiny boy with neat blond hair. She'd heard how his health had worsened after a couple of days, how Bridget had begged the nuns to send for a doctor for William, how it had taken a further sixteen days for William to be sent to hospital and how he'd died less than three weeks after that. Bridget wasn't allowed to see him and she wasn't told where he was buried. She was told he had a congenital defect but Bridget has always believed this wasn't the case.

Like Joan, Bridget had made a new life for herself in London; she'd got married and reared three children, but had also been admitted to a psychiatric hospital and had attempted suicide three times. And she had also struggled to get information. In the mid-1990s, Bridget returned to Bessborough to ask about how William had died and where he was buried. The nun who met her led her down the avenue, on to a small path, towards the Angels' Plot. She tapped her foot on a small unmarked patch of grass. 'Your baby is buried there,' she told her, but she said Bridget wouldn't be allowed to put a marker there to remember William.

The first thing Joan thought of when she heard the news about the commission's interim report was how upsetting it would be for Bridget. The report had revealed that an infant whose details corresponded with William's had not in fact been buried in Bessborough; he had been laid to rest in Carr's Hill Cemetery, a former Famine burial ground, in an unmarked grave, the grounds overgrown with wild barley and clover. After they read the relevant paragraphs, Bridget and her family had had to battle with the commission, and then the Child and Family Agency, in order for a letter proving William's place of burial to be released to them. All along, the congregation had the information Bridget had requested more than two decades before but she had never been told the truth. In the prefab classroom, Joan gave her a smile of encouragement but Bridget looked visibly shaken.

When the speeches were over, Joan finished her tea, but the anxious feeling had started to grow. I can't stay here much longer, she thought. She said her goodbyes but back in her car she felt depleted, and the journey home took every ounce of energy. In her flat, her mind harked back to the sound of the door slamming behind her, the smell of polish, that first lonely evening in the dormitory with the other girls. Maybe it's too much for me to go back to Bessborough, she told herself. There is just so much loss, so much sadness. It's not a place where I can find healing.

Chapter Nineteen

CORK, 2020

The garden had had an especially good year, Joan thought, looking through her patio doors at the pots of sunflowers and freesias and the hanging baskets full of sweet pea. It had got more attention that summer, now that lockdown had stalled her routine of community groups and meetings and women's sheds. It was a small space, but with some bunting left over from a party and a blue-and-white tablecloth over a patio table, she'd made the best of it.

Coco the terrier gave a small yelp. 'Sssh,' she told him, picking up her iPad. A new Facebook notification had just popped up.

'You're only a young one, Joan,' it read. She laughed.

Joan had posted a photo of day three of her 10,000 steps

a day challenge and her friend Claire was cheering her on. Claire was always one of the first to interact with her posts; she liked Joan's lockdown memes and Irish dancing videos, her pictures of walks with her grandchildren in the woods. In turn, Joan liked Claire's posts about initiatives to save bees, the best crab claws in her county and support for nurses.

She checked her emails. Walter hadn't responded to the last message she had sent, a while back now. Things had changed since that first year, when Joan had wanted to play catch-up, had wanted Walter to be involved in everything. And for a time, he was. At Julie's fortieth birthday celebration, he'd sat beside Joan's brother, laughing and joking; with only ten years between them, they looked more like brothers than uncle and nephew. This is what it's all about, Joan had thought then. Having all my family in a room together.

As time went on, they'd met less often, but she'd still felt a strong connection. And Walter would still surprise her if he was nearby. 'Mam, I'm down your way, I'm going to pop in. Put the kettle on for a cup of tea,' he would text her. And he had a good relationship with Julie too; he would call in on her occasionally. In the winter, he would bring her a bag of turf for the fire. And yes, Joan knew they were different; as a family, Joan and Julie and Emmett had spent decades in London, and Walter was rooted in a rural farming community. But it didn't matter; they got on well together.

Some distance is a normal part of the process, she reminded herself. She clicked the 'Like' button on Claire's reply. Claire was going through the same thing, navigating a reunion with her own son. Maybe when lockdown is over I'll head west, she thought, looking through Claire's recent post of a west coast beach, with its golden strand and the sun peeping through the clouds to give a spectacular glimpse of the mountains.

'Do you have the same relationship with Walter that you have with your other children?' Claire had asked her once, when she'd phoned to have a chat.

Joan had taken a second to respond. 'No, I don't,' she'd admitted. 'It's a totally different love.' She hadn't really said that out loud before, hadn't allowed herself to tell it to another person. And sometimes when she thought about the other women she knew who still hadn't found their children, she had pushed that thought to the corners of her mind.

'My relationship with Walter will never be the same as with my other two,' she'd told her. 'I would be kidding myself to say that it could be. I love Walter to bits. And I love my other children. But Julie and Emmett, I have a different love for them than I have for Walter. I can't describe what the difference is. But it's not the same.'

And as Claire had listened, Joan had suspected that perhaps she'd asked her the question because she struggled to articulate the same feelings herself.

'I've had Julie and Emmett from birth. I've been there when they were sick. Their first day of school. I know every inch of them. I know that my son Emmett doesn't take butter, I know the chocolate he likes, I send Kimberley biscuits out to where he lives in South Africa to him. And I know my Julie takes a sweetener in her tea, so that's why I keep some here for her. But with Walter I had to ask him if he took sugar in his tea. I love him – he's my son – and I always will, but I didn't rear him. I have to get to know him … If I don't hear from him for a while, my mind will go into overdrive. And my Julie is a great philosopher. She'll say, "He might not want to move at the same speed as you …" So I'm being a bit more open and considering the impact all this is having on him. Then when he does ring he says, "Ah, no, Mam, don't be giving out. Look, I know, I know I should have rung …"'

Claire had taken her time to respond. 'Thank God you said that, Joan,' she'd told her. 'Because I feel the same way.'

And as they'd ended the conversation and promised to speak again another day, Joan had felt the special relief that came from speaking to someone who understood her.

A couple of months later, when the hanging-basket blooms had almost disappeared, Joan had shared another Facebook post, a quote from a site she visited from time to time. 'I admire people who choose to shine even after all the storms they've been through,' it read. And Claire had responded, 'That's you and I,' she wrote. 'Indeed Claire, how strong we are,' Joan had replied, throwing in two biceps emojis for good measure. Others too had started to chime in with comments, leaving a flurry of likes, good wishes and hearts.

The quote had spoken to her because the pain of what she experienced would never fully go away. She would always feel a sense of loss; it was something no amount of yoga videos or guided meditations or walks by the sea would get rid of. But recently, she'd felt a sort of acceptance, a sense of calm. She was so glad Walter was in her life, in whatever capacity he wanted to be in it. When he'd responded to Joan a few weeks back, he'd called her on her mobile and it had been one of the best chats they'd had in ages.

As she put down the iPad, her eye rested on the photo on her sideboard, next to the television and the vase of flowers from her garden. It was a photo of her three children, in a decorative white frame, and that one image seemed to capture all the complicated emotions she felt. It had been taken against a plain-coloured background the last time Emmett had come home to Ireland to visit. Julie was in the middle, with her cropped dark hair and a black top, and the two men were either side, both wearing striped shirts in bold colours. They were convulsed with laughter, beaming at the camera as if they'd never been apart.

Part Two

TERRI'S STORY

Chapter Twenty

15 OCTOBER 1979

It was 6.15 a.m. and already Terri wondered how she could get through the day. Even now, six years on, this day was a struggle. So many hours stretched out in front of her until she could go to bed again and put it behind her for another year. She grabbed her dressing gown and tiptoed downstairs, wanting to savour the few precious minutes before the children woke up and the day began in earnest.

In the kitchen she flicked on the kettle, made some tea and arranged a tea cake on a plate. Then she placed a candle on top of a little plastic holder and lit it with a match. She watched the flame burn for a few seconds, casting its shadow on the cake's spongy surface.

She looked at her watch. It was 6.30, the time he'd arrived into the world, bewildered and covered in blood.

'Happy birthday to you,' she sang quietly to herself.

Niall would be six today. Six whole years apart from Terri. Two thousand, one hundred and ninety days that she had spent wondering about where he lived, who gave him his dinner in the evening. Five whole years of this little ritual, celebrating his life by herself. It got harder as the years went on, her mind trying to conjure up images of him in school now, learning to read, maybe even riding a bike.

A wail descended from upstairs, baby Louise* starting to stir, demanding a feed. Terri yawned, rubbing her eyes and trying to shake herself awake. She'd tossed and turned the night before, telling her husband she was alright, that she'd nod off in a minute. She tipped the rest of her tea down the sink and blew out the candle, the small spiral of smoke rising through the air and then disappearing.

Chapter Twenty-One

DUBLIN, 1972

Terri took the pipe cleaners out of her red-brown hair and arranged it around her narrow shoulders, satisfied with the extra volume. Then she unscrewed the bottle of black mascara and applied it to her lashes top and bottom. With the right make-up, she could look older than her seventeen years, and she knew she'd have no trouble getting served. She rummaged around for a long chain. She'd wanted to look extra nice that night – she was going to a gig with the girls from the supermarket and she'd been looking forward to it all week.

She was so lucky with her colleagues from H. Williams. She had made firm friends with a group of the girls from the minute she started working there; there was always someone nearby to joke and laugh with while she stacked packets of tea and biscuits. Terri had taken to the job – she had an easy way with the customers. No one in the supermarket thought she was as thick as two planks or rolled their eyes at her if she didn't know something. It didn't matter to anyone there that she wasn't as academic as her two older sisters and wasn't going to shine in exactly the same way they did. If reading labels was a bit difficult, it didn't matter: she could remember where things were by the colours on the packets.

Grabbing her jacket downstairs, Terri looked in on her mother in the sitting room, waving her goodbye. Outside, the air had a hint of the freshness of a late summer's evening and her platforms made a satisfying clacking sound on the pavement. She loved wearing them. They transformed her four-foot-ten-inch frame into a respectable five foot three, and they looked good under her flared jeans that she had tie-dyed in the bath.

Passing by the green, she hurried up the narrow street along the row of terraced two-storey houses. She'd have to get a move on – she'd heard the band were good and she didn't want to miss any of their set.

In the pub, Terri sorted herself out with a glass of Harp and joined the rest of the group near the stage. She loved nothing better than live music. She played the piano and wrote her own songs. Her father played in his own band when he was finished his shifts in the bakery; he'd inherited that gift from his own mother, who had mastered so many instruments Terri had lost count.

The local band were making a commendable stab at Neil Diamond and Leonard Cohen tracks. The singer had power in his voice – Terri had to hand it to him, he was pretty decent. Moving closer to the stage, Terri could see that he was a good showman too, lapping up the attention from the crowd. He was tall and dark, while beside him the guitarist had a young face but his hair was a pure, icy white. After a few up-tempo tracks, they switched into one of Terri's favourites, Kris Kristofferson's 'Sunday Morning Coming Down'. The singer wasn't quite Johnny Cash, but he had a convincing quality, that trick some singers have that can make you feel like the song is just for you.

At the interval, he tapped Terri on the back. 'I'm Phil*,' he said.

'Terri,' she replied, shifting awkwardly on her platforms.

Up close, he was better-looking than on stage: his hair was thick and curly, and his eyes were kind. His lines were a bit cheesy, but they worked.

For the next few months, Phil and Terri were inseparable. They went to the pictures, to cafés, to discos and to every gig in the city they could manage. Terri didn't feel shy about playing some of her own piano music for him; she told him how songs would pop into her head when she least expected it and she'd have to scrabble around in her bag for a pen and paper before she lost any of the magic. And Phil couldn't get enough of hearing her stuff.

'You can write songs for my band, Terri,' he said, only half-joking. 'And we can go on tour.'

Terri loved to imagine it, leaving Drimnagh's washing lines and narrow streets behind and climbing into a van with Phil and the guitar cases, travelling to dancehalls and pubs all over the country.

And if she was honest with herself, Terri liked being out of the house, away from the rows between her mother and father, the empty whiskey bottles, the way the atmosphere could go from calm to unpredictable in a split second. It was as if she had two fathers: one was the quiet, intelligent man who earned a wage the other men on the street could only dream of, the man who bought his wife a new car. The other was bitter, snide, nasty. 'You've nothing upstairs, Terri,' he'd tell her. 'You'll have to figure it out yourself,' he'd say to her when she asked him for help with her homework. 'We don't know where we got her,' he'd joke to his friends. But her mother had it worse, and Terri sometimes wondered if she was afraid of him. 'Have your own money,' she'd always told Terri. 'And carry yourself like you're royal, even if you haven't got a penny.' And she and Terri never discussed it, never said a word outside the house, never let on what was really going on inside the house with the colour TV.

'Are you sure you're alright with that fella?' said the girl behind the counter. Club A Go-Go in Abbey Street was filthy, smelling of sour beer and sour bodies, but it had the best music in Dublin. Phil was unsteady on his feet; it was the point in the night when he'd downed so many pints that he lost all sense of where he was. Terri knew she'd have a job to get him home.

'I'm grand, don't worry. He'll be embarrassed tomorrow when he wakes up.' The girl didn't look so convinced and Terri flashed her a smile as she guided him out of the club. She didn't care what people thought. Phil was gentle and caring and, besides, no one went through life without picking up a few faults along the way. And she knew from her father that this was the way these musicians behaved; it was part of who they were.

'I'm sorry, Terri,' Phil slurred. 'A guy I knew from playing gigs kept buying me pints.'

At least it was just the drink, she reasoned. He didn't touch any of the other stuff passed around in the clubs, she had to give him that. No, Phil was a decent soul, even when he'd had one too many. The drink never brought out the darkness in him that she'd seen in her father.

Chapter Twenty-Two

LONDON, 1973

Terri wrapped her scarf and coat around her. In north London, the frost formed an icy patchwork on the pavement near her aunt's house in Palmers Green. She'd arrived not long after Christmas, looking forward to a fresh start in a new city, a clean slate. 'I make friends easily, I'll be fine,' she'd told her parents and a despondent Phil. 'And I can stay with Auntie Paula* until I find my feet. Her husband is away a lot with the navy, so she might like the company.' Her mother was all for it; she'd loved London the few times she'd gone over to visit her sisters. She'd miss Terri and Terri would miss her, but she'd said that some time away would be good for her; experience in London would stand to her when she came back.

At the bus stop, Terri checked her watch. She had just enough time to pop into the corner shop. Getting a job had been so easy; she'd sorted one after a couple of days, a supermarket job in Wood Green, a short bus ride from her aunt's house. It was bigger and better-stocked than any place she'd worked in Dublin, but the job was essentially the same: stacking, helping out on the floor and being pleasant and efficient with the customers. They'd put her on the checkout, and she loved chatting with the regulars; she just laughed when they teased her about her accent or joked about how she pronounced certain words. Maybe in a few months she'd move out and into a flat with girls her own age. Perhaps she'd even get that job in Marks and Spencer she'd applied for and she'd take the Tube every day into the big flagship store in the city.

Paying for her cigarettes and a bar of chocolate, Terri felt a familiar bout of queasiness. Sometimes she got so caught up in her plans in London that she forgot the real reason she had upped sticks from Drimnagh. She'd missed a period and she prayed it would be a false alarm. From the little bit she'd learned from her friends, she knew what it might mean but she hoped and prayed things might resolve themselves. She'd missed one before and everything had been fine; it had only been the one time with Phil. But if her father found out, he'd be furious at her, and Terri knew the person who would suffer would be her mother, who fundraised for the local church and sprinkled herself with holy water every time she left the house. So she'd bought a ticket for the boat as quickly as she could – she hadn't even told Phil the real reason she was so hell bent on London.

Settled at her till, her new tray installed in the machine, Terri hoped she could get through the morning without needing to stop.

'Are you alright, love?' asked her colleague at the next till.

'I'm grand, nothing to worry about,' she reassured her. For her own sake, she hoped she was right. She'd give it a couple more weeks and then she'd go to the doctor.

In the hospital near Palmers Green, Terri sat on the edge of a bed in a busy emergency ward, wincing at the pain in her back. She'd skidded on a toy lorry that one of her little cousins had left on the stairs, landing with a thud on the hall carpet. Auntie Paula had heard the full force of the fall and insisted she go to the hospital.

The doctor was kind, examining her thoroughly. Terri didn't pay much attention, the pain and the shock absorbing her thoughts.

'You haven't broken anything but your back is bruised and you need to rest,' he told her. 'But you'll be fine. And the baby is fine.'

There it was, he'd confirmed it. In a way, Terri was relieved. At least she knew for sure. In a few months she was going to be responsible for a little person. The doctor talked about options, told her about procedures that could be done if she wished, but Terri couldn't take it in.

'I'll leave you to think about it,' he said, pulling back the curtain to reveal Auntie Paula. Seeing her face, Terri knew she had heard.

'You wouldn't have a procedure done, would you, Terri? You wouldn't do that, would you?'

'Please don't tell my mother,' Terri begged her. 'I'll have the baby and sort myself out, but please don't tell her.'

Her aunt nodded. Terri didn't know whether to believe her or not.

The noise of the ward made it impossible to rest; through the thin curtains Terri could hear all of her neighbours' chatter with visitors and nurses doing the ward round. She heard the whoosh of the curtain being pulled back and a woman with a clipboard sat down by Terri's bed. She was youngish, with a brisk manner, and Terri was surprised to hear an Irish accent. She wanted to fill out some forms, she told her; Terri assumed she was some kind of hospital administrator.

'When did you arrive here, Terri?'

'About a month or so ago. I've started work in a shop in Palmers Green.'

'Are you married?'

'Yes,' Terri lied instinctively. Best not to let it get out that she wasn't married.

'Where is your husband?'

'He's up north on a job. His boss sends him all over the place.' She hoped she'd been convincing enough.

'And when is he coming back?'

'I'm not sure; when the job is done, I suppose.'

Then there were more questions, about who her husband was and whether he was Irish, and Terri didn't understand why any of it made a blind bit of difference and had to be included on her hospital records. There was something about the woman's tone and demeanour that made Terri feel like she had done something wrong; when the woman turned to go, Terri was left with an uneasy feeling that she couldn't shake.

❖

A week or so later, healed after the accident, Terri turned the key in the lock of her Auntie Paula's house. She could hear unfamiliar voices in the kitchen and the conversation came to an abrupt halt as she closed the door behind her.

'Terri, love. Come into the kitchen for a second.'

A priest and two nuns were squeezed into the small space, sitting around the table with a cup of tea.

Terri wished she could light up a cigarette and steady herself. Something had felt off since she'd come back from the hospital a few days ago. In the evenings, she had heard Auntie Paula's hushed voice on the phone, when her aunt thought she was out of earshot. It was obvious she was talking about Terri, but she couldn't really make out the words. And sometimes, even when she was being so kind to Terri, running her a bath or bringing her some tea, Terri felt that she wasn't quite meeting her eyes when she spoke to her.

The priest looked at her. 'Terri, you do realise you cannot stay in this country?'

'What do you mean I can't stay? What did I do?'

'You have to leave, I'm afraid.'

'But I've got a job here, I'm working. I don't want to go back now.'

'Your bag is packed and you have to go home to Ireland. All of the arrangements have been made.' He turned to Terri's aunt. 'It's time for us to go,' he told her.

Terri looked at Auntie Paula. She seemed tense, her face pinched with worry.

'It's for your own good, Terri. It's for the best. You'll get great care.'

Did her mother know? And her father? Had they all agreed to this?

One of the nuns picked up the brown leather suitcase that her aunt had packed and put it into the boot of the car outside.

'They're good people,' Auntie Paula told Terri. 'It's the right thing to do.'

The priest grabbed her by the arm and Terri got in. No one spoke to her, offered her a tissue, asked her if she was OK. When one of the nuns mentioned the sign for Heathrow she understood she was heading to the airport, and soon the car pulled up outside the departures area.

Walking up the metal steps to the plane, Terri froze, the priest grabbing her roughly by the arm again. The air hostess looked right through her, greeting the other passengers and checking their tickets.

In her seat, Terri put her head back against the leather headrest and took a deep breath. She felt as if she was watching herself in a film, as if she were an outsider seeing her own story unfold. She heard an American accent; the woman in the next seat was chatting to someone in the next row about it being her first trip to Ireland.

Then she turned to Terri. 'Are you OK, dear?'

Terri mumbled something about being afraid of flying. She was sweating; she knew she probably looked pale and out of sorts.

'Just take it easy, it's a short trip.'

Terri nodded, trying to steady her breaths.

'Where are we going?' she asked the air hostess.

'Cork,' she replied, moving swiftly down the aisle, not pausing to notice the confusion plain on Terri's face.

When they'd said she was going 'home', she'd presumed they'd meant Dublin. She'd never even been to Cork.

Then she heard the roar of the engine and felt the plane ascend into the sky. From the window, she watched London get smaller and smaller until all she could see were the clouds.

Chapter Twenty-Three

BESSBOROUGH, 1973

The car zigzagged down a country side road, and as it slowed, Terri could see two large pillars with iron gates, but she couldn't make out a sign or a house number. Another nun, called Sister Paul, was driving; she had picked Terri up from the airport and refused to answer any of her questions. As they got to the end of a long drive, a huge Georgian house came into view. What struck Terri was how intimidating it looked, or at least the outline of it she could see in the faint evening light.

'This is it,' announced Sister Paul.

Exhausted, Terri picked up her brown case and followed her up the stone steps.

A heavy red door slammed behind them as they entered. Terri took in the house's wide hallway, its gleaming parquet floor. Quick little footsteps approached and she could see a small, slight nun with a youthful face walking towards them.

'Stay there, you can go into the office when you're called,' she told her. Sister Paul exchanged a few words with the nun and left without saying goodbye.

On one side of the hallway, a door was slightly ajar. Another, older, nun beckoned Terri to enter.

'I'm the mother superior,' she said, giving Terri a cool stare. The desk and table looked grand, made of a solid, expensive-looking hardwood.

'Name, please.'

'Terri.'

'Don't be stupid. That is not a name.'

'It is my name, sister, everybody calls me Terri.'

'I'll find your real name,' the mother superior said, fishing around in an envelope and pulling out a letter. 'Your name is Teresa. But never mind that for now. Your house name will be Tracey. And your house number is 1735.' Then she waved Terri away with her hand, her expression making it clear that there would be no further discussion. In the hallway, Terri stood by the huge wooden staircase, which looked like it went on for miles. Her mouth felt scratchy and she wanted a drink of water.

A few minutes later, the small nun reappeared.

'Follow me,' she said. They climbed up flights and flights of stairs to the top floor, where Terri could see a long dormitory with a high ceiling; there was a small bedside locker beside each iron bed.

'You can have this one,' the nun told her, pointing at a bed in the corner.

Another girl, also pregnant, was lying in the next bed with her back to them. She didn't make any effort to turn around or look at Terri.

'I'll be back to allocate you your work and tell you where to report,' the nun said, turning on her heel and leaving the room.

'Can I please have some water?' Terri called, but the nun had already left.

Terri sat on the bed; she stared at the brown case she didn't recognise. Her aunt must have packed it, folding in the few dresses and cardigans and bits of underwear. The thought of it made her so angry. As she'd packed it, she must have known that Terri would be sent to this place; she must have known that this was the plan.

Another girl entered the dormitory and gave Terri a faint smile, the first kindness anyone had shown her all day, but Terri couldn't bring herself to smile back.

The nun returned a short time later, taking in Terri's still-packed case.

'Why have you still got your coat on? Have you not sorted yourself out?' She sighed. 'You'll have to do it later. Come on.'

Terri couldn't muster the energy to protest. The whole house, it seemed, was a maze of stairs, echoey corridors, pale walls. At the foot of the big staircase, the nun led her down a hallway to the back of the house, then through a door leading to the yard. Outside, the ground was paved, then they went down some more steep stone steps into a basement laundry.

'This is where you'll report for duty tomorrow morning,' she said.

Terri took in the long sheets, the overpowering smell of detergent, the damp, musty smell of this airless room. Her heart sank, thinking of her job just a few days before, sneaking cigarettes at breaktime, the women from east London she had a laugh with, the pensioner who dawdled at her till and refused to be served by anyone else.

Back in the dormitories the other girls had gone to bed. The nun returned with a bottle and instructed Terri to have a urine sample ready in the morning. Terri didn't ask what it was for. She was too drained to ask any more questions, to allow her thoughts to race around her head, to wonder, to worry, to speculate. All of that could wait. She slept in her clothes, too tired to pull the covers up around her.

Chapter Twenty-Four

BESSBOROUGH, 1973

Terri scoured the inside of the heavy pot with steel wool, scooping out the remainder of the morning's porridge that clung to the edges. It was thankless work, and sometimes she struggled to lift the pots, but at least it was better than the laundry. She'd tried her best there, but with her small frame, she hadn't the strength to wring out the heavy sheets and after a few days the nuns had decided it was best for all concerned that she be moved to kitchen duty. She'd hoped there'd be more time to chat there too – in the week she'd been in Bessborough she had rarely spoken to anyone – but even here, the other girls kept to themselves, getting through their shifts without a word. Maybe they were right, Terri sometimes thought, what was the point of making all that effort when they couldn't even tell each other their real names?

She dried the pot and left it back up on the shelf. She felt woozy, weak.

'Bridget,' she whispered to one of the other girls, 'I've had a bit of bleeding and I just thought it was like a period. It's probably nothing, but I just wanted to ask someone.'

Bridget's face was grave. 'I don't think that's supposed to happen when you're pregnant. You need to speak to the nuns about that.'

'I haven't really spoken to any of them since I arrived.'

Bridget looked her squarely in the eye. 'We all try to keep out of their way but this could be serious, Tracey– you have to.'

Terri's cheeks reddened. It was another one of those things she should have known but didn't.

At lunchtime, she approached one of the nuns. 'Sister, I have some bleeding. Something is not quite right.'

The nun barely looked up from her work. 'Go out to the grotto and pray. Pray to God to forgive you for your filthy sins.'

Terri thought of the doctor in England, the lengths he had gone to to ensure that she understood everything, and she wished with all her heart she could go back there. Was it dangerous? she wondered. Would everything be OK?

❖

'Tracey,' said a voice. It took Terri a split second to realise that she was being addressed, and when she turned around in the large kitchen, she saw that a member of the congregation was trying to get her attention. 'You've got a visitor. They're waiting for you in the visitors' room.'

Who? Terri wondered as she muttered a brief thanks. In the few weeks she'd been in Bessborough, she hadn't left the institution, hadn't got to know anyone in Cork, hadn't got in contact with any of her friends or family. She put down the saucepan and wiped her hands on a tea towel. A visitor was at least a break in the routine of mass, meals, work and bed.

Downstairs in the small, plain visitors' room, she could see a round face and big black-rimmed glasses familiar to her: Sister Paul. The nun gestured to the seat opposite her, and in the afternoon light Terri saw that her skin was smooth; she was younger than she'd realised.

'Tracey, I hope you've settled in.' Her eyes betrayed no warmth or concern. 'I'm here to talk to you about your case.'

What case? Terri thought. She just wanted to go back to England. 'When am I going back, sister? There's been some kind of mistake.'

'I can assure you, Tracey, that there's been no mistake of any kind.' Her voice was calm, assured, authoritative. 'You can't go back to England while you are pregnant.'

Terri tried again. 'But I shouldn't be here. I want to leave.'

Sister Paul wasn't angry. Her mouth curled up at the edges, almost as if she were amused.

'What are you talking about, Tracey? You're being looked after here by the sisters. You'll have your baby here and I will oversee the adoption. There are plenty of lovely families lining up.'

'It's my baby. I want to keep my child.'

'No, no, that's out of the question. Just think about it, Tracey. Where are you going to live? How are you going to provide for this child? You should be thankful.'

Why should I be thankful? Terri thought. She never asked to come here, never asked to be shut away from everyone, scrubbing pots and pans from one end of the day to the next. But she stopped herself before the words came out of her mouth; she knew she couldn't lose her temper with a nun.

The questions continued, about Terri's background, her father's occupation, her mother, her hobbies, her home life, her siblings. Sister Paul took notes, carefully writing down each point. Terri answered each one, afraid to challenge her.

Sister Paul got up to leave. 'Remember, Tracey, no one must know about what happened to you. Nobody,' she said, making her way towards the door. As she stopped to chat briefly with another nun, Terri heard her tone of voice change and it seemed lighter, warmer than the one she had used with her. Terri made her way back to the kitchen to finish off the rest of the dishes, Sister Paul's questions reeling in her head.

❖

In the evening, when the stacks of dinner plates were rinsed and tidied away, Terri slipped outside. It was May and the weather was just starting to turn towards summer, the last of the spring flowers vanishing, the bright evenings making it harder to sleep. She headed towards the grotto, to the statue of the Virgin Mary with her blue-painted robe, protected in a stone-walled enclosure, ivy growing at the top. As a child, Terri had always been taught to pray to her, and she stood there for a few moments intoning the familiar lines, hoping it would quell the anxious feeling in her stomach.

Behind the grotto, she spotted a dirt track in the ground. She'd never followed it before, never ventured much around the grounds, but the route brought her towards a stream, the water lapping against the stones and glistening in the last rays of the evening sun. She wondered for a second if she might be able to swim across, what might await her at the other side of the water's edge.

On the way back to the house, the caretaker gave her a curt nod. He was smoking, the earthy smell of his lit cigarette taunting her. She hadn't had one since she'd been in London.

'Can I have one?' she asked him.

He nodded, offering her the packet and fumbling around in his pocket for a light. Something about his demeanour suggested to Terri not to bother him too much with conversation, but the simple act of taking a puff and allowing the nicotine into her bloodstream settled her nerves for the first time in weeks.

A few days later, on a Thursday afternoon, she was called into the little downstairs room again, expecting to see Sister Paul. This time, it was a younger woman, not much older than herself, with long dark hair. She smiled as Terri approached.

'Tracey, I'm Mary,' said the woman, reaching her hand out to shake Terri's. 'I volunteer to visit the people whose families don't come to visit them.'

Terri nodded. She hadn't written to any of her friends or family so there was no chance they were going to come and visit her, like some of the relatives of the other girls did. She still didn't know for sure if her mother had been told she was back in Ireland.

'I've brought you something.' Mary passed a bottle of shampoo across the table.

'Thank you.' Terri was glad of it – it looked like a decent brand.

Mary's tone changed: it became more businesslike. 'Have you thought about what's going to happen to your child?'

How could Terri think of anything else? Sometimes on Sundays, she did parlour duty, bringing in trays of tea and biscuits to couples who had come to inquire about adopting a child. All Terri could think about was which poor girl from her dormitory would have to leave without her own baby and it made her want to smash the tray on the ground.

'I want to keep my child,' she told Mary.

'Tracey, what kind of life would they have? You have nothing.'

Terri looked at her, willing herself not to let her emotions show on her face.

'There's your own future to consider too. Don't you want to get married and have a family of your own? You won't get a husband if you already have a child.'

'Why are you saying this to me? I don't know why you are saying this to me.'

'I'll leave you to think about it, Tracey.' Mary got up to leave, but she didn't head out to the front entrance, as visitors normally would. She headed towards a back door used by the girls and there was something about the surety of her footsteps that suggested she knew the layout of the place very well.

'Mary, did you live here before?' Terri called after her.

Mary continued towards the exit. Had she once been in Terri's position, shut away in a big house with visits from people she didn't know? Had she herself done what she advised Terri to do and placed her child for adoption? Would there be more visits like this until Terri relented? As she made her way back to the kitchen, Terri made up her mind that she had to write to Phil and tell him everything.

When Terri was called downstairs again at the end of May, Phil's face beamed at her from the other end of the table. Seeing him made her think of all the things she used to enjoy in Dublin, the gigs and the parties and the music, and she blinked back tears.

'I'm so sorry, Terri. I came as soon as I got your letter.' He looked distraught, his eyes full of concern for her. 'I'd have come before if I'd known. It'll be alright, Terri, don't be worrying.'

Thank God for the caretaker, Terri thought. Just this once, he had told her, as he folded the envelope into his pocket when she'd gone on another evening walk, promising it would go out in the following morning's post.

'It's nice outside,' she said. 'Let's go for a walk. I can show you the grounds.' She looked at the nun on duty, who nodded.

Outside, she couldn't hold the tears in any more. 'I can't stay here, Phil, I can't be here any more.'

'I'm so sorry,' Phil kept saying.

They did a couple of circles around the grounds, walking past the greenhouses where some of the girls worked, past the front lawns and flowerbeds and down the avenue where the afternoon light filtered through the leaves. When they got to the front gates, Phil stopped and turned to face Terri.

'Come on,' he said. 'I can't leave you here in this place. We'll go back up to Dublin and we'll work it out.'

Terri grabbed his hand and followed, walking out of the institution, seeing the outline of the city in the distance.

Bessborough 1970–80

It is remarkable how much Terri remembers about her experiences and her interviews are full of clear, arresting detail, her warm voice occasionally breaking in her home in north Dublin. She is physically tiny, her eye make-up carefully applied on a face that's still youthful; when she laughs I can almost see flashes of what the teenage Terri might have been like. One of life's extroverts, she thrives on chats with others, updating me on runaway dogs and songs she was playing on the piano, inquiring about my family, a recent job application, whether I had been called for the Covid vaccine.

Terri's interest in people extended to volunteering and decades of campaigning. Before the pandemic, she'd run a choir for people she had met when she was a volunteer board member of the Christine Buckley Centre, an organisation for survivors of institutional abuse. When I joined her for tea and custard creams in her cottage in Dublin, she'd been getting over a spell of spinal surgery, walking with some difficulty with a crutch. But she'd still found the energy to join Zoom meetings, petition government ministers and speak with members of the collaborative forum – a group set up to facilitate dialogue between the state and survivors of mother and baby institutions on issues relevant to them – that she had been involved in.

Like Joan, Terri spoke out because so many others she knew could not do so. From the outset, she made it clear how important the language used in this book was to her. For her, the terms 'former resident' and 'mother and baby home' were not appropriate, as she felt they were too soft in terms of the experiences she and others went through. 'If we're trying to inform and empower the public, and raise awareness of the truth, we must describe it properly,' she explained to me once. Similarly, she rejected the term 'birth mother'; she said it was not her choice to not be allowed to raise her son after his birth.

Terri's descriptions of being returned to Ireland against her will stayed with me long after our first interview. I thought of her as a bewildered young teenager as I ploughed through academic articles, interviewed historians and looked through old newspaper archives to try and find out why it happened. Terri too was keen to read and inform herself about it as much as possible. And once I sent an email attaching some documents and academic articles I had collected, I knew she would sit at her iPad that evening, poring over them, trying to understand why she had been returned to Ireland against her will.

Reading through the historical information I could access, I could see that, as early as the 1920s, charities in England began to write to the clergy in Ireland criticising pregnant Irish women who had travelled there.[12] Looking through the reports of the Department of Local Government and Public Health in the National Library, I saw that by the 1930s complaints about 'the number of girls who having got into trouble leave the Free State and go to England' had been recorded. The complaints also started to find their way into the press, embarrassing the fledgling Irish state. In 1936, journalist Gertrude Gaffney wrote in the *Irish Independent* about 'the girls who have run away from Ireland to hide their shame ... all concerned feel it unfair that they in England should be saddled with the expense and worry of them'. Gaffney also claimed that Irish women were availing of the services of Protestant rescue societies.

In response, government officials proposed a repatriation scheme in 1931. Under the scheme, pregnant Irish women seeking assistance in the UK would be encouraged to return home and the Irish government pledged to cover 50 per cent of the repatriation costs. From the 1940s, most repatriations were overseen by the Catholic Protection and Rescue Society of Ireland (CPRSI), an organisation founded in 1913 to prevent Catholic children from being adopted by non-

Catholic families. There are repeated references to the faith of Catholic children being in 'danger' in the annual reports of the CPRSI.[13]

The number of women being repatriated rose steadily in the 1950s and '60s. Some women refused to return but were sometimes put under pressure to do so, with officials threatening to inform their landlord or their employer; sometimes the journeys they were pressured to take put them at medical risk.[14] Social workers were said to have used the term 'PFIs', pregnant from Ireland. Children born in England to Irish mothers were also repatriated. Local authorities worked alongside the Department of Health, the CPRSI or organisations such as St Anne's Adoption Society, based in Cork, to place Irish children born in England in Irish homes. From the late 1960s, St Anne's also repatriated women before they gave birth, sending them to Bessborough or in later years placing them with families in the locality.[15]

Repatriations reached their peak in 1967, the year abortion services were introduced in England. From the late 1960s, references to abortion are more frequent in official documents and the CPRSI warned of an 'added and very grave danger' which placed a 'temptation of a very serious nature before the distraught unmarried mother'.[16] The numbers of Irish women availing of abortion services increased, and by 1971 the CPRSI stopped recording repatriated women in their annual accounts, though repatriations did continue to be carried out by smaller organisations and adoption societies, such as St Anne's.[17]

Terri thinks she may have been one of the last women to be repatriated to a mother and baby institution in Ireland in the twentieth century. She still has lots of questions about how her repatriation was arranged and funded. She says her son's adoption was organised through St Anne's Adoption Society, so it is possible that the society arranged her repatriation also, or perhaps it was informally arranged by the CPRSI. She does not know who the woman who visited her bedside in hospital was, though she now suspects it was an employee of the CPRSI or St Anne's Adoption Society, who then contacted the priest and nuns who arrived at her aunt's house. 'Their attitude was, you can't stay in this country, this country's not going to pay for you, you've nowhere to go so you'll have to come with us,' she told me.

By the 1970s, mother and baby institutions in other countries were closing. Within Ireland, attitudes towards single mothers were also starting to change, albeit at a much slower pace. In 1973, a group called Cherish was set up in Dublin by single mothers Maura O'Dea and Colette O'Neill. From O'Dea's sitting room, the group lobbied the government for more support for single mothers and their children. That same year, an unmarried mothers' allowance was introduced, and four years later, the Employment Equality Act gave women legal protection from being dismissed from their job during pregnancy. When I asked Terri about the allowance, she said that at no point was she made aware of its existence. 'Never, never ... there wouldn't have been a whisper of that,' she said.

Alternatives to mother and baby institutions were also being proposed in Ireland in the 1970s. Organisations like Ally and CURA placed women and girls with unexpected pregnancies with families rather than in an institutional setting. The families did not receive payment for providing accommodation, though there was an expectation that the women and girls would do housework or look after children. Despite this, the numbers of women admitted to mother and baby institutions remained high. Over 2,500 women were admitted to Bessborough in the 1970s, the highest number of admissions for any decade, and the average stay for women admitted there was less than ninety days.[18] Like Terri, many of those admitted would have been in their late teens, with the same lack of knowledge about or access to contraception, which wouldn't be made legal until the end of the decade, and even then only for married couples.

Though attitudes had started to soften, the changes came too late for Terri and the women and girls she was in Bessborough with. I thought of her and the culture she was sent back to as I came across an article written in the *Irish Independent* in 1972, just a few months before she passed through Bessborough's doors. It described the institution as 'Cork's banishment house', housing women and girls from thirteen to forty years of age. The matron, Sister Hildegarde, told the newspaper that 'the unmarried mother is no more acceptable to society than she was 50 years ago'. The article stated that some women and girls had attempted a variety of abortion methods, including a girl who had been so distressed at the news of her pregnancy that she had ingested sheep dip compound in the hope that her baby would be born dead.

After Terri left the institution with Phil, she found her way to the train station and on to a relative's house, whose identity she does not wish to reveal, expecting to stay there for a few days until she and Phil could find a new place to live. But the relative contacted her mother. 'I remember my mother coming and saying, "Come on, it's time for you to go" ... I think I just shut down,' she recalled.

Phil was sent home and Terri was driven to another mother and baby institution, this time St Patrick's on the Navan Road, not twenty-four hours after she had walked out of the gates of Bessborough.

Chapter Twenty-Five

ST PATRICK'S, 1973

On Saturday evening, one of the nuns in St Patrick's mother and baby institution called Terri downstairs. The place was huge – even bigger than Bessborough – and sometimes Terri wondered how she could have gone through eighteen years of her life living just a short drive away without hearing so much as a whisper about it.

'Tracey, you're to ring home,' the nun told her. Terri stood beside her at the payphone in the hall, dictating the number. 'Hello,' the nun said. 'Are you prepared to take a trunk call?' After a short pause, she passed the phone to Terri, not moving from the spot. Terri heard her mother's voice at the other end of the line. She willed herself not to cry.

'How are you, Terri? How is it all going in London? Are you still having a great time?'

Her voice was thin, strange. The nun remained in the background, nodding at Terri.

She took a deep breath. 'I'm fine, Mam,' she began, though both of them knew it wasn't true. 'Working hard.'

It never used to be like this; they never struggled to find things to say to each other. At home, Terri was always the one who got on best with her mother. Even as a teenager she never tired of her company; she still went with her to the supermarket, didn't mind doing the dusting and wiping and cleaning with her at weekends. Now she just wished for the call to be over. She heard her father's voice in the background asking to be put on to her, the fear that crept into her mother's voice.

'She can't stay long on the phone – it's costing her a fortune to ring from London,' she heard her mother tell him. 'I'll tell her you said hi.'

Hanging up the phone, Terri remembered the last conversation they'd had, or lack of, on the way to St Pat's when she'd come to collect her. And Terri hadn't protested about going there; she had seen the look of disappointment in her mother's eyes. It was so odd, she and her mother and the nuns colluding in these lies. It made her feel lonelier than ever, knowing that her mother was aware of everything but that she and Terri had to go on pretending.

It was surprising, really, how many things in St Pat's were exactly the same as Bessborough: it too was a rambling old building, red-brick this time, Terri had kept the same house name – Tracey – she'd been reassigned to kitchen duty, and she still slept in dormitory-style accommodation with others. St Pat's had the same echoey sound, voices that bounced off high ceilings and large rooms. Other things were different: the grounds were smaller, and in St Pat's she always ate meals with the same group of girls, around small round tables which were cleared away for arts and crafts in the evenings. So far Terri had avoided speaking to anyone.

At breakfast the next morning, Terri's feet were itchy and tight; they'd swollen so much that she could barely put her shoes on and they pinched her heels.

'Tracey, isn't it?' said the girl sitting next to her. She had a tangle of dark curly hair and her voice had a soft Northern Irish lilt. Terri nodded. She hoped she would leave it at that; her feet were killing her and she didn't want any small talk. But the other girl soldiered on. 'We hear you're a blow-in from Cork – you've got that special social worker,' she teased. She meant Sister Paul; some of the other girls dealt with a lay woman in a tweed suit. She was from a different adoption agency in Dublin; Terri was starting to learn that a network of agencies worked with each institution.

Terri gave a half smile, noticing the girl's round, expressive eyes. She felt mean for being so standoffish – the other girl was only trying to be friendly.

'I told my social worker I'm getting married after this but I'm not sure she believes me,' the girl said. For the rest of the breakfast, Terri heard all about Jimmy, her boyfriend, who had said that they'd get engaged, would find a little place to live together with the baby. It would all work out, he had told her.

For her sake, Terri hoped it would. She hadn't dared to contact Phil or write to him from this new institution. There was no point, she thought. She wasn't going to put either of them through all that again.

In the afternoon, Terri was called in to play the piano for the nuns in the small room they used as a private recreation area.

'Very nice, Tracey, very nice,' said one of the sisters.

Terri smiled to herself. Her fingers, raw from kitchen duty, had still found their way around the ivory keys with the same fluidity as always. The nuns hadn't noticed the changes she had made to the original arrangement of the 'Ave Maria'; from memory she couldn't quite recall all of it, and she'd put her own spin on the music, swapping notes here and there to make it interesting, making sure not to clash with the accompanying chords. She played a couple of other hymns she thought they might like, and they chattered softly in the background, occasionally stopping to praise her. She thought of the ferocious nun who had taught her to play; she'd pulled Terri from classes to make sure she got weekly lessons and could read sheet music; she remembered how her father secretly listened outside the door when she played.

After a while, Terri stopped enjoying it, the requests for hymns and parlour favourites irritating her. Why am I here playing the piano when I shouldn't be in this place at all? she asked herself. Finishing the notes of the final song before it was time to go, she vowed to herself that if they asked her to play the piano for them again, she'd make up some excuse about why she couldn't do it.

Chapter Twenty-Six

ST PATRICK'S, 1973

In September, Terri could feel a chill in the long hallways of St Pat's. In the tiny, spotless chapel, she pulled her cardigan around her as she positioned herself by the altar. She hoped she wouldn't be too uncomfortable during the baptismal ceremony; her baby was due in just a few short weeks and she didn't want to stand for too long.

Catriona, the girl from Northern Ireland, had had her own baby, a boy, a few days earlier; she'd named him after Jimmy. Terri had wanted to refuse to be godmother. She was starting to develop an aversion to masses and ceremonies, the prayers she said, the things she had always believed. But Catriona had seemed so excited to ask her. 'You're one of the only real friends I have in here,' she had told Terri. 'And one of the only people I've shared my real name with.' And Terri hadn't the heart to say no – Catriona really believed that she would go back home and get married to Jimmy and come back and claim her son. 'He's mine,' she had told Terri, 'and they can't take him away from me if I don't want them to.'

In the chapel, baby Jimmy fussed slightly and Catriona straightened the christening outfit around him; there was one in St Pat's that all of the girls used and Catriona had been so thrilled to dress him up in it, making a memory. As the ceremony was about to begin, one of the nuns muttered to Terri, 'He'll be baptised by his new mother and father anyway. It's ridiculous.' Terri knew she was right; the baby was going for adoption and would most likely be baptised again by the adoptive parents in their local church, but she wished the nun hadn't said it within earshot of Catriona.

She looked at her friend, who was using every ounce of effort not to let it show that the comment had bothered her. Terri felt for her: she just wanted to do this one thing for her child and now the moment was spoiled by a cruel remark. She could see the tension in Catriona's face when she said Jimmy's name, when the priest anointed his head with oil, when he placed the first few droplets of water on the child's forehead, when they lit the christening candle and welcomed the church's new member into the fold.

❖

On a Friday evening in October, there was an event for the girls in a back room, with music playing on the record player, a few balloons, some cakes and buns. Terri thought she would enjoy the break from the usual crochet she did in a circle in the evenings, making ponchos and blankets and christening shawls, but all through the evening, she felt fragile and light-headed. She put it down to tiredness – these last few weeks it had been difficult to sleep. On her way back to the main house, she noticed a trickle of blood-tinged fluid running down her leg.

'Stay there and I'll get help,' one of the girls told her – in her confused state she didn't know who. Terri positioned herself on the step, confused, all of her energy suddenly drained from her body.

A short time later – Terri didn't know how long – she heard quick footsteps approaching her; it was a nun she didn't know and her expression was serious.

'Come on, you'll have to report to Sister Elizabeth and we'll see what's wrong.'

The walk across the yard to the annexe at the other end of the institution seemed to take an age, and Terri could barely manage it, stopping to steady herself every so often. In a small room with some lounge chairs and a table she waited for Sister Elizabeth, wondering if this was the start of labour and what on earth was in store for her.

❖

After six days of waiting, Terri was restless. She'd found Sister Elizabeth to be capable and competent; she'd put Terri on bed rest in a long dorm with other empty beds but nothing had happened yet. If there was still no sign, Sister Elizabeth had told her, she'd go back to the main house. Terri hoped she'd go into labour soon, she wasn't looking forward to being back on kitchen duty again, not when it was so hard to move around, so difficult to rest.

That evening, Terri's waters broke, soaking the bed with fluid, and she knew she was in labour. One of the night nurses brought her into a small room with a steel trolley bed. She was left on her own. Occasionally one of the two nurses would look in on her; the door was left ajar and she could hear snippets of their conversations. The pain started lower in her abdomen, but as the night went on, it seemed to grip all of her body in twisting waves.

Saturday and Sunday brought more and more pain.

'Please get Sister Elizabeth,' she asked the night nurse, a lay woman with black hair.

'Would you ever stop; we don't wake the sisters at night.'

'Please can you ring my mother or a doctor or somebody?'

The nurse just sighed. 'You won't be in such a hurry again the next time, will you?'

Terri's eye stung with tears. She was in such pain, bleeding heavily, and the sheet was badly stained; the sight of it frightened her. Through the window, she could see the light changing to dark, and again the first rays of morning light. Sweat poured down her body; nothing she'd heard from her friends or aunts or older relatives had prepared her for this.

Terri felt weaker and weaker, as if her body was being emptied from the inside out. In the early morning, she gave a final push and a loud, confident cry filled the small room. There was her baby boy, wriggling, covered in fluid and flecked with white; she thought her heart would burst. Then she felt her body tremble again, and she heard one of the nurses say her blood pressure was low.

'Call an ambulance,' said another. 'She's in shock.'

Terri felt scratchy tinfoil being arranged around her, the soft screeching sound of it being moulded into shape. Her head banged off the table. She made out the blurry shapes of a series of people gathered around the bed, and then she felt strong arms lifting her onto a stretcher and into an ambulance, driving fast through the city. When she woke up, in a strange bed surrounded by plastic floral curtains, a nurse told her she was in St Kevin's Hospital. But she didn't have the energy to ask any questions; she just noticed the occasional nurse or doctor coming into check on her as she drifted in and out of sleep.

Chapter Twenty-Seven

ST PATRICK'S, 1973

Baby Niall gulped down his bottle. In St Pat's annexe, where she had been since she had been discharged from hospital, Terri hummed the notes of a new song that had come into her head a while back. She could have sworn that Niall liked it – he seemed to settle when he heard it, his little mouth gripping the bottle even more tightly. The bottle finished, she picked him up and put a blanket on her shoulder to wind him. She loved every minute of it, these hours with him; she could feed him, bathe him, change him, examine his tiny knees and fists, his tufts of hair and sallow skin. He wasn't like the other babies she had seen before; to her he was distinctive, a one-off, with his dark eyelashes and soft pillowy cheeks. The other girls were sent back to work a couple of days after the birth – only allowed to see their babies at feeding time – but Sister Elizabeth had determined that Terri could stay in the annexe for two weeks until she recovered.

She heard the shuffle of footsteps and she looked up to see one of the other girls, due to have her baby very shortly. Terri waved her over; she was dying for someone to see Niall. So far the only person to coo over him was herself.

'Do you want to have a look at him?'

The other girl oohed and aahed over him and Terri felt a burst of pride.

When the girl left, Terri put a new babygro on Niall, a little lemon-and-white one that looked so nice against his skin tone. One of the girls was going to come in with her camera later and she wanted Niall to look his best for the photo. She cuddled him close to her, kissed him on the top of the head.

'No, don't do that.' The reproachful voice of a nurse reached her from the other end of the dorm. 'It's not fair on the baby and on his new mother when she gets him.'

Terri kept her eyes downward. First they'd forced her to take the tablets to stop the breast milk, but now she wasn't even allowed to hug her son to her? She busied herself by propping Niall up against a little peach baby seat, the lining decorated with tiny yellow ducks and blue rabbits. That too would look nice in the photo, the colours matching Niall's tiny yellow babygro. She wondered if Niall would still be her son when the photo was developed or whether she'd be forced to give in to Sister Paul.

❖

'Tracey, there's a nun up from Cork in the nursery.' Mary, one of the girls on stairs-cleaning duty, had come into the kitchen. From the landing, she had a good view of visitors coming in and out of St Pat's, and she'd taken it upon herself to tell the others if she saw anything unusual. Terri set down the mop in the bucket of soapy water and looked up at her.

'Sister Paul?' Terri remembered their last conversation only too well, Sister Paul pushing the paper across the table, Terri trying not to lose her cool and not rip it to shreds. As firmly as she could, Terri had said she didn't want to sign it and Sister Paul had done little to hide her irritation.

'It's the same one that was here before. She must have been waiting for you to come back from the annexe.'

For the rest of the morning, Terri went through the things she might say to Sister Paul. She could say she needed more time and be polite, or she could simply say that she didn't need to sign anything because she was Niall's mother. He was five weeks old now, so alert, his eyes open and ready to take in the world around him; she felt that he knew her, that he recognised her when he saw her.

At feeding time, she hurried from the kitchen to the nursery, past the lines of cots to where Niall's was. His cot was empty, the little wrinkle in the mattress and the babygro and blankets rolled up at the end of the cot the only signs that he had been there. Her son was gone, and no one had even thought to warn her.

'Where is he?'

'It's the best thing, Terri, it's in your best interest,' said a nun.

But the tears came and kept coming, a mixture of shock and grief and humiliation and shame.

'Tracey, for your own good, be quiet,' whispered another girl.

Terri didn't care. She imagined Sister Paul lifting the blanket she had crocheted for him, taking off the clothes she had dressed him in that morning, dressing him in new ones, removing any trace of Terri from him, preparing him for another family, another mother that wasn't her.

Chapter Twenty-Eight

DUBLIN, 1974

'Terri, it's Catriona.'

Since they had left St Patrick's, Terri and Catriona had defied the rules about not revealing their true identities and had kept in touch via letters and phone calls.

'Catriona, how are things?'

The last Terri had heard was that Jimmy hadn't kept his promise and Catriona was arranging to leave Ireland and stay with her aunt in America. Sometimes Terri envied her; Terri was back in Drimnagh, working in Superquinn, trying to avoid the worst of her father's moods and the digs from her relatives about not having come home to visit when she was in London.

'Terri, I couldn't wait to tell someone. I'm going to get baby Jimmy back.'

'Oh my God, Catriona, that's amazing! ... But you can't just walk in and take him, can you?'

'Yes, I can, he's my child. And I haven't signed anything. Even if I had it wouldn't matter until the adoption order is issued. It's the law. The social worker doesn't like it, she'd already organised an adoptive family for him, but he's my son and I want to keep him. I'm going to get him in a couple of weeks.'

'I'm so delighted for you, Catriona, I really am.'

Catriona gave her a brief, excited goodbye and Terri hung up. She could hear the hum of the TV from the sitting room but she went straight upstairs; she couldn't bear to have to make small talk with her mother and father and keep her voice even and calm. Her mother never mentioned Niall or Bessborough or St Pat's and her father still didn't know she'd been anywhere except London. She couldn't bring herself to contact Phil after everything that had happened. How could she possibly do what Catriona did and take Niall back?

A few days later, Terri took a moment to gather herself by the walk-in storage fridge in Superquinn. She thought no one had noticed her, but then she heard a voice asking if she was alright. It was Darina*, a friend of a friend, married to Ronan*, who Terri knew from Drimnagh. Darina worked in the supermarket too; she was easygoing, good with people, the way Terri supposed she used to be too.

'I'm fine, don't worry about me,' she said.

'Are you sure? You seem a bit distracted.'

It was true, Terri was more distant than usual. She couldn't think of anything except the conversation with Catriona. Her head was filled with different images of what it would be like to go to the adoption agency in Cork and bring back baby Niall. But then after that, her mind went blank. She couldn't picture bringing him back to the house with her father, and who was going to rent a flat to a single mother?

'The thing is ...' she began. And then she surprised herself by starting to talk, her sentences tripping over each other as she told Darina the whole story from start to finish.

On her next day off, Terri rang St Anne's Adoption Society and was greeted by a voice she didn't recognise. She steeled herself. She had to be firm.

'I want to collect my son, Niall,' she began, surprising herself with the confidence in her voice. 'He was born in October. I dealt with Sister Paul in Bessborough and St

Patrick's and I'd like to get in contact with her so I can take him back. There will be three of us coming to collect him.'

Thank God for Darina, she thought; she and her husband said they'd put her up in her spare bedroom until she could get herself sorted.

The nun had listened politely and they'd settled on the date for Terri to travel to the agency's offices in Cork City.

'Thank you, sister,' she said, putting down the receiver. She meant it too; the woman hadn't reacted at all in the way Terri had expected. After all the months of worrying, all she had to do was make one phone call to be reunited with Niall.

She picked up the phone again; she'd ask Darina to come shopping with her and get a few bits for him. Maybe another yellow outfit, she thought. It would be really nice against his dark hair.

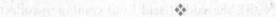

The early train from Dublin to Cork was about to leave and Terri, Darina and her husband Ronan hurried onto the nearest carriage. It wasn't a particularly pleasant morning, drizzly and miserable in a way only March days in Ireland can be, but Terri couldn't have cared less. She imagined Niall, five months old now, responding to people and starting to enjoy life. In just a few hours she could see it for herself.

'Thanks so much,' Terri told them. 'I feel so much better having you with me.'

The offices were down a narrow street in Cork City. Terri's hands shook as she knocked on the door. Sister Paul answered, giving them a stern look, and Terri felt her excitement vanish.

'Are these people related to you?' she asked Terri, nodding towards Darina and Ronan.

'No, we're her friends,' Ronan blurted out.

'Well, then they have no business coming in if they are of no relation to you or the child.'

Darina and Ronan gave Terri an apologetic glance and stepped away from the door. Privately, she admonished herself for not thinking of it, for not saying they were her sister and brother-in-law.

Inside the small office, Sister Paul took her seat behind her desk and was joined by a priest. Terri looked around for a carrycot or a Moses basket, but she couldn't see anything.

'Where's Niall?' she said. 'I said I was coming to collect him.'

'He's settled now. He is with his mammy and daddy who are looking after him.'

'But I'm his mother. I said I wanted to take him back.'

'How did you think for one second that I would allow that to happen?'

Terri clenched her hands tightly together under the table. 'But—'

The priest nodded. 'If you decide to do this, Terri, we'll have to tell your father in his place of work.'

Sister Paul picked up the phone. 'And that won't be the last of it. If you continue with this, I'll have a lot of phone calls to make,' she told Terri. 'First, I'll ring the papers and you'll be all over them tonight for trying to take a child away from a decent family when he is settled in with them. Then I'll ring our solicitor and tell him what's going on. And you better have plenty of money because it's very expensive to go to the High Court.'

Terri bit her lip. She didn't want any of this, her name splashed over the papers, her father finding out like this. And how would she get the money for solicitors? She'd spent the little she had saved on the new stuff for Niall.

She tried again. 'But I just want my son. He's mine.'

Sister Paul's voice rose in volume as the conversation continued.

'You're not getting him back, Terri. You have to get that idea out of your head ... and if you don't get out of my sight, I'm going to make another phone call. This time to the guards.'

Terri picked up her bag and hurried out of the office, tears stinging her eyes.

In the street, she waited for Darina and Ronan in the drizzle. They came back after a few minutes, their faces furrowed with confusion to see her on her own.

'I thought you told us he was yours, Terri,' Ronan said.

'He is, he's my son.'

'He couldn't be – you must have signed him away or something. Otherwise they'd give him to you. They couldn't just take him like that.'

Terri couldn't bring herself to explain, to try and muster the energy to make sense of it. They got the evening train back in silence, the bag of clothes for Niall shoved under a seat.

❖

In May, Terri's mother called her into the kitchen. By then, Niall was more than six months old, Terri kept count in her head.

'Sister Paul was on the phone from the adoption agency,' she told her. Her voice had that same tone she'd used at Christmas, when she'd found Terri crying in her room and told her to fix her make-up and come downstairs. 'She said that you have to sign those papers. There's a place in town you have to go to.'

'I'm not signing anything.' She hadn't told her about her trip to Cork and her encounter with Sister Paul.

'You have to, otherwise they'll send the guards for you. I can drive you if you want.'

'You're not driving me anywhere, I'll go in myself.'

In the days that followed, her mother didn't mention it again and Terri spent as much time as she could outside the house, avoiding conversation, avoiding confrontation. She didn't go and sign the papers, and if her mother got any further phone calls, she didn't mention them. Terri wondered if they'd ever get their closeness back or if all that remained between them was distance and bitterness and disappointment.

Chapter Twenty-Nine

DUBLIN, 1976

Terri pressed the button in the shower and savoured the sensation of the hot water on her exhausted body. Her baby girl, Susan*, was one day old and soon she'd be able to take her home to the little flat in Harold's Cross she shared with her husband, Peter*, whom she'd met through a friend in the supermarket. Moving under the shower stream, she winced. The birth had been difficult; she'd been diagnosed with placenta previa and was on bed rest for most of the pregnancy, trying not to think about all the things that could happen.

The doctors and nurses had been so kind, but her discharge date couldn't come soon enough for Terri. She and Peter had been in a motorcycle accident when they'd only just met, when a drunk driver crashed into them, knocking Peter off the bike and sending Terri into a ditch. She'd spent time in intensive care and endured months of hospital rehab. They'd married a couple of years ago, Terri in callipers and Peter's arm in a sling, the priest looking them up and down and asking which war they'd been caught up in. With hospital being such a big part of her life the past couple of years, now she just wanted to be in her own home, playing the piano for baby Sue and watching her tiny body drift off to sleep.

She slipped a clean nightdress on and made her way back to the ward. When she reached the cot she felt her stomach turn over. Little Sue was gone.

'My Sue's not here. They've taken her.'

'It's alright, Terri, the nurse took her for a second.' Mary, another patient, had been keeping an eye on Susan while Terri showered. Her voice was calm but Terri couldn't take it in. For a second, she got a flash of that morning in St Pat's, the empty cot and the blankets rolled up at the end of the bed.

'She's not here, she's gone,' she said again. Her breath came in short, shallow bursts that didn't seem to be giving her enough oxygen. Though it was only a few seconds, it seemed like an age before the nurse appeared in the doorway with Sue in her arms, safe, calm and asleep.

'Terri, it's alright. She's here. Did you think I was going to run off with her?' she said, smiling.

Terri felt her cheeks burn as she took Sue back in her arms.

'Don't mind me,' she told her. 'My mind is all over the place. I don't know what's wrong with me.'

But that night in her hospital bed, she clutched Sue to her, not wanting to set her down. It had been such a long road to have her own baby in her arms, and she couldn't relax just yet.

A few months later, Terri woke up clammy, shaky, out of breath. She'd had another nightmare. It was always the same one. She would hear a baby crying, but it wasn't Sue. And she wasn't in the flat: she was in a large, rambling house with lots of staircases, the sound echoing off the high ceilings and magnolia walls. She would feel a draught and would run down a corridor which led to another. The cries would get louder, and Terri would knock on door after door to try and reach baby Niall but would get no answer. And then she would wake up and realise that, though the dream was over, the anxious, unsettled feeling remained.

She lay there, listening to her husband's deep breathing as he slept. He knew all about Niall; she'd told him everything from the moment they'd started going out.

'Where can we go to get him?' he'd asked her when they'd

got engaged. 'We'll find him,' he'd assured her over and over again. He didn't mind that Niall wasn't his; together, the three of them would be a family.

'It's too late,' she'd told him. And it had taken a while for him to accept that they couldn't go back now, not after all that had happened and the threat of the guards hanging over her. Since then, he hadn't asked any more questions and Terri didn't talk about it. When a programme came on the television about a lost child, he changed the channel, both of them keeping their eyes fixed on the screen.

Chapter Thirty

DUBLIN, 1977

Terri gathered up the sandwiches wrapped in tinfoil, the togs and the sunhats and put them into a big hold-all. Then she scooped up baby Sue and settled her in the pram. It was her first day at the sea – she and Peter were taking her for a day out at Mosney beach. Terri couldn't wait to introduce Sue's little velvety feet to the sand, to take her down to the water to dip her toes in it.

At the beach, she set the blanket down on a patch of sand, laying Sue down in the shade. She and Peter stretched their legs out in the sun, grateful for the few moments of peace, the picnic they could have later at their leisure. The trip to Butlin's was the first holiday they'd had together as a family, and after all the time Terri had spent in hospital, they were glad of the break, a chance to do normal activities again.

After a while a young couple their own age with a little boy set their blankets and bags down on a nearby patch of sand. The boy got excited and tried to squirm his way out of his mother's arms.

'Niall,' she told him. 'Wait a minute.'

Niall. The little boy's name was Niall. It couldn't be, could it?

Terri forced herself to keep still, not to crane her neck and stare. But behind her sunglasses, her eyes fixed on that child. He was dark-haired, like her own Niall was. He looked about four, the same age Niall would be now. She couldn't see his eyes, what colour they were, but she could tell this boy was lively, well able to talk. She scrutinised the couple too; they were energetic, friendly. Their accents sounded like they were from Cork; could her own Niall be living in Cork? Would it be odd if she tried to start a conversation with them? Would they think she was a bit off if she asked them about the child's birthday to see if it was the same as her own Niall's?

She looked at Sue, tried to redirect her thoughts, but she knew it was pointless. There had been other times like this, incidents that threw Terri off-kilter. It was as if Niall was her shadow child, always following her around, always out of reach. And she too was a shadow Terri, a part of herself shut off from those around her. She watched as the little boy ran off with his father to take a dip in the sea, his brown hair glistening in the sun.

Chapter Thirty-One

DUBLIN, 1982

Terri ushered Sue, Brian* and Louise* into the church, taking her seat in a pew beside her sisters and her nieces and nephews in the top rows. Her mother's coffin was just a few feet away. It was cancer, alarmingly quick. Her mother had come back from a holiday in Spain and people had remarked on her great colour, but a doctor had thought it was a little off. The tests showed it was a rare disease of the bone marrow, too far advanced for anything to be done. A few months later she was gone. She was fifty-one.

Terri only caught snippets of the sermon, the usual platitudes about how generous her mother was, how devout, the devoted mother and granny she had been. But Terri couldn't bring herself to think about how her mother polished Terri's piano until it shone or about the trips to London they'd taken together when Terri was a child, Terri's eyes widening at the double-decker buses and the pristine red-brick buildings. Instead, she thought about all the things that had festered, the times Terri had told her mother that she couldn't get down to Drimnagh, but soon, soon, when she had time, she'd come. And then when she did go she'd avoid being in the same room with her; she'd duck out for a tea or a cigarette; she'd never make any conversation beyond small talk about the kids. She'd tried, but she could never forgive her for what happened with Niall.

Sometimes Terri thought her mother had struggled too, that there was something on the tip of her tongue she wanted to say to Terri but couldn't find the words. And now they'd never talk about it. She'd never tell her mother that the silences between her and her husband Peter got longer and longer every year. Or that sometimes she raced to the door when the bell rang because, in a dark corner of her mind, she thought that someone would be calling with news of Niall.

The smell of incense reached her nostrils as the priest said the final blessing. She watched as the men picked up her mother's coffin and carried it solemnly out of the church.

Chapter Thirty-Two

DUBLIN, 1992

Terri stared at the photocopied pages from her adult education class. She had an essay to write for English, due in the next couple of weeks. She yawned, exhausted from the night before. The late shift in the Jacob's biscuit factory ran until eleven, and then she got up early the next morning to shepherd Sue, Brian and Louise off to school. She'd also been picking up some double shifts, racing around from school to supermarket to factory.

At least the classes were in the morning; she could fit them in around late shifts. She'd initially signed up for Inter Cert English and then Maths, and when she'd sat and passed those exams, she'd signed up to do her Leaving Cert. Getting started on the assignments was the problem – it was always tricky to write the first couple of lines. When she got going she was fine.

She flicked the switch on the kettle. A cup of tea couldn't hurt. The presenter's voice boomed from the radio in her kitchen. She could hear him switching to a new segment as she stirred the tea, and as she took the first sip, he was introducing a woman who was doing research into adoption. Terri set down her tea with a bang, turning up the radio. She'd heard the words 'pilot study'. The researcher, from a children's charity, was looking for participants, women whose children had been adopted and who might be willing to talk to the research team. Anonymity was guaranteed.

Terri reached for a pen and paper, took down the number and folded the paper away neatly in a drawer. It was time, she told herself. Niall would be nineteen now; she'd carried out her little ritual with a cake on his birthday every year. And sometimes she still imagined she saw him in a flash of her mind's eye; it had happened a few summers ago when she took the kids out to Portmarnock beach. For a second she had seen a grown-up Niall chasing the younger children in the sand dunes, his skin tanned from the sun, before disappearing as quickly as he had appeared.

Maybe the researchers could help her: maybe she could write to him, trace him somehow. Maybe it would help her to stop feeling so disconnected; even with all the effort she put in to her work, to raising her children, to improving herself, she couldn't help feeling that she was going through her life in a bubble, its cloudy filter separating her from the world around her.

Terri didn't find the research project itself that helpful, but through speaking to others she'd found out how to contact the adoption agency and had spoken to people who had been through the same experience as her. A few months later, she arranged a meeting with some of the mothers she'd met. She was happy with the small, plain room in the North Star Hotel. Tucked away, it wasn't likely to be mistaken for a conference room or for a party, so they'd be unlikely to be interrupted. They'd call themselves a book club.

She dragged a few chairs around in a circle, the metal legs screeching against the floor. She checked her watch. Almost 7 p.m. About to start. How many would come? she wondered.

'Terri,' said a voice. It was Maura*; she'd walked in from her place in town. Terri breathed a sigh of relief. At least one other person had come. Then a woman with wavy hair, then another woman with a sleek bob trickled in, followed by one or two others.

'I'm glad to see all of you here today,' Terri began. 'I know it must have been difficult to come.' There were women from

Bessborough, but also St Pat's and the other institutions she'd come to learn were dotted around the country.

She went through the introductions and invited the others to speak.

'I'm just happy to talk to people who understand,' began Julia*, one of the older women. 'I can't talk to my husband or to my family ... when it happened all those years ago my brothers said I couldn't tell anyone about it, that it couldn't get out ... Then when I came back, nobody said anything ... It's made it really difficult to trust anyone, to feel like anyone is on your side, or even to feel close to anyone else ...'

Some of the other women nodded in agreement. Watching them, Terri was reminded that she wasn't the only one, that others, too, had spent years feeling like they were utterly on their own. Lately, between going back to education and meeting people in a similar situation, the layers of shame that had built up inside her brain had started to loosen and lift, allowing her to understand that what had happened to her had never been her fault.

Chapter Thirty-Three

DUBLIN, 1998

In the corner of the lobby of Wynn's Hotel in Dublin, Terri nursed a cup of tea. She was exhausted, always tired these days, running to meetings and community events and projects at the National Women's Council. And it had been busy on the Parentline helpline that week: she had answered so many calls from families in distress.

Still, she didn't regret leaving Jacob's and taking voluntary redundancy, not for a second. When her friends from work heard she was leaving, one of them had phoned Peter and asked if she was alright. 'She can't be right in the head if she's walking away from a job like that,' they'd said. And in a way they weren't wrong: she had three kids to feed and a mortgage to pay. But one evening as she looked around at the huge hot ovens, the conveyor belts, the bins for the discarded biscuits, she knew in her heart that she couldn't spend the rest of her years in a white cap, breathing in the smell of processed sugar. And Peter had understood, in his own way, though they were growing more and more distant by the day.

She'd found the Shanty Educational Project a couple of months after that. She'd boarded a bus in Tallaght with her cousin, the bus driver rolling her eyes at them when Terri had asked if it was really a cult. Over the next few months, Terri attended classes and events in community development, sociology and spirituality, her mind opening and stretching in all directions, the bubble she'd disappeared into for so many years growing fainter and fainter. She'd built up to a BA in Applied Social Sciences, winning a scholarship to cover her fees. And she'd also attended counselling, learning about red flags, everyday things that could bring back the bad memories.

She willed herself to stay alert. Her friends kept telling her she was taking on too much, working all the time, saying yes to everybody and everything and filling every hour in the calendar. But when her friend Maria* had called her and asked her to sit at the other side of the lobby while Maria met her son for the first time, Terri didn't have the heart to say she was busy. 'I'm terrified,' Maria had told her. 'I just want to know that there's somebody there if things go wrong.'

Would I want someone else around if I was meeting with Niall? she wondered. She suspected she wouldn't; she'd prefer things to be private, to save the moment just for the two of them. Since she'd been involved in the pilot study with the researcher a few years back, she'd written to the adoption society, and they'd told her that her son was alive but that she'd have to wait a bit longer to pass on requests. And the kids knew everything now – before too long she might even have all of them in a room together, having a meal as a family.

She looked up from her tea and glanced across to the other side of the lobby. Maria had clearly made an effort, with neat hair and a hint of subtle make-up. Terri hoped she was feeling calm, that her jitters weren't getting to her too much. After a few minutes, she saw a young man arrive, sit in the chair opposite Maria and smile at her. Terri returned to her tea, it wasn't right to observe them too closely, to take away any part of the experience between Maria and her son. A few minutes later she glanced up again and she could see them chatting together, joking, with animated hand gestures.

She smiled, making her way towards the door, and she saw Maria waving her over. She'd say a brief hello and leave them to it. Watching them gave her hope; maybe one day soon she'd laugh like that with Niall, as if they'd never been separated.

Chapter Thirty-Four

DUBLIN, 2001

Una took a deep breath and there was a long pause. 'My God, Terri, you've never let on.'

Una was the sister of a woman Terri worked with on a charity helpline. A social worker, Una was the first person Terri thought of when she read in the newspaper that St Anne's Adoption Society was closing. The files were being transferred to the health board. Niall was twenty-eight now, and she'd still heard nothing. It was time to try a new tack.

'No, I've never had reason to open up to many people, I suppose ... Una, I hope you're wearing your professional hat because I'm going to ask you to do me a huge favour if you can. I tried so many times with St Anne's but they kept putting me off. Would you try to make contact with him and see if he would agree to meet me?'

'Terri, these things can be very complicated, but I promise you I'll do my best.'

Terri thanked her, hung up and exhaled deeply. Una was discreet, kind and gentle and Terri knew she could trust her. She wrote another long letter to Niall, asking again for it to be put on file.

A few weeks later, Terri's mobile buzzed while she was at work. It was Una.

'Can you talk?'

'Of course.' Terri put the 'Do not disturb' sign on her office door.

'Go ahead,' she said, sitting back down in her chair.

It took Una a split second to get started, but to Terri it felt like an age, she shifted uncomfortably in her seat.

'Terri, he's very like you,' she said.

'Oh God.'

'He's lovely, a really lovely fella. I interviewed him for over an hour. Everything is fine, he's well, he's healthy, he has had a good life and all the rest of it.'

Terri could sense a hesitation in her voice, but she really hoped she was wrong.

'I hate to tell you bad news, Terri, you know that ...'

'I know.'

'He doesn't want to meet you. Not at the moment. He said he just can't afford to go there.'

'He actually said that, those words? "I can't afford to go there"?' It was an expression she used all the time, when she didn't want to face up to something or when she knew a situation wasn't in her best interests.

'He did.'

Terri blinked back tears. 'My God, the number of times I said that.'

'I tried my best for you, Terri, I really did.'

'Do you think he'll change his mind?'

'Terri, I don't think so. I'll be honest with you, he said that he didn't wish you any harm, that he had no ill feelings towards you.'

'Did he ask anything about me?'

'No, Terri, he didn't. He didn't want to know details about you.'

Terri thanked Una for all she had done and ended the call. At her desk, she stared at her computer and the pile of papers. She felt so jealous of Una, who had been in a room with her son for a whole hour, who could look him in the eye, who saw what he looked like, had examined his facial features, heard his voice. Terri was his mother and she'd never get that opportunity. That was all the information she was going to get. She knew that Una couldn't tell her his name or any personal details that might identify him. He'd never see the letters she had put on file for him. He'd never know her side of the story, and she'd never get to explain.

Chapter Thirty-Five

BESSBOROUGH, 2014

Michael put his indicator on, turning into the driveway past the big stone pillars, the rows of trees and the white fence-posts. He parked in front of the old house and Terri felt herself break out in a cold sweat. The old white conservatory was still there, in need of a lick of paint. It was her first time back to Bessborough in over forty years and the first thing that struck her was how so many things had remained the same.

She'd met Michael more than ten years before, not long after she separated from Peter; she'd admitted to herself that she and Peter weren't compatible, that perhaps they shouldn't have got married at all. With the trauma of the motorcycle accident heaped on top of Terri's distress at losing Niall, perhaps the relationship had never really had a shot.

She closed the car door, Michael giving her a worried glance. 'Let's go for a walk,' she told him. 'I want to show you where I used to go.'

Together, they followed the tree-lined path down to the small graveyard marked with iron crosses for the nuns. The graves were well-tended, the grass cut low, and she spotted new markings, one for a baby who had died in the 1990s. By a small stone sculpture she didn't recognise of a mother and child, visitors had left teddies, flowers and stuffed toys in memory of the children who had died.

She kept going; she wasn't ready to be still. In the background she saw the old stone folly, a landmark of so many of her evening walks. The grotto was still there too, covered with mature ivy. The paint was weather-beaten, the face of the statue worn and aged by the years. She looked for the track behind it, where once she gazed out over the water and wondered where it would lead her. Instead she found a gate; some of the land had been blocked off and redeveloped, absorbed into the urban sprawl.

'Terri,' said a voice. She turned around to see the BBC's Fergal Keane with his producer and cameraman. 'Thank you so much for doing this,' he said.

It had been hard to find someone to do a TV interview, Terri knew that. She hadn't volunteered herself, but when another Bessborough mother she knew from Facebook had asked her, she couldn't bring herself to say no. So many women found it difficult to speak out, fearing they'd hinder a reunion, but in the past thirteen years there'd been nothing to suggest that Niall had changed his mind. 'I'll do it,' she had told her. 'I'll be a voice for others.'

As the team set up the cameras and explained how things would go, Terri reminded herself to remember Niall's birthday, 15 October 1973. If he's watching, he'll hear it, she told herself, and he'll realise who I am.

'He vanished into a black pit. Just a black pit,' she told Fergal. 'It's like his life was stolen. And mine ... His birthday comes round every October on the fifteenth. He was born at 6.30 in the morning, he weighed six pounds six ounces and he was beautiful, he was beautiful.' Tears spilled down her face as she recounted her experience. When the interview was over, she sat on the rocks behind the folly, rushes and wild grasses in the background. Fergal and the team had been kind, but the interview didn't bring her any relief. She felt emptied out, sapped of all her energy. I have to go, she told herself.

That evening, as silvery clouds pinkened overhead and Michael opened the front door to her house in Dublin, Terri put down her bag and headed straight for the piano. It had followed her to every flat and house she had lived in since she'd moved out of her parents' home in Drimnagh; on the top she kept the photo of Niall as a baby, in a yellow wooden frame. She composed a melody in less than an hour and as evening turned to night she played it for hours until she felt calm again.

Chapter Thirty-Six

DUBLIN, 2020

In a recovery room in north Dublin, Terri woke up in a fog of medication. She'd had emergency surgery for cauda equina syndrome – where the nerves in the back become severely compressed and can cause paralysis – but the drugs hadn't masked all of the pain. It was dark; she couldn't reach for her phone or her iPad to check the time. She could remember only snippets of what had happened earlier: nurses and doctors rushing around, their faces hidden by PPE. 'The ward is locked down due to Covid-19. We can't let any visitors in,' one of them had said.

Terri looked around. The curtains had been pulled around her bed, blocking her view of the ward. Her thoughts darkened. For a second, she was reminded of the floral plastic curtains of St Kevin's Hospital, when she'd woken up after that difficult birth with Niall almost five decades ago. The room started to spin and she felt as though a heavy weight were pressing down on her chest, blocking her airway. One thought wouldn't go away. *I'm on my own, I've lost control.* She called for a nurse.

'I want you to call my partner. I want to get out of here,' she told her.

The woman paused. Though Terri couldn't see her face through the PPE, she expected that her expression was blank, confused.

'I need to get out now,' Terri pleaded. That thought again. *I'm on my own, I've lost control.*

'We'll get the doctor for you,' she said.

The doctor on night duty sat by her bed, talking to her calmly, until the medication started to kick in and she succumbed to sleep again.

A few months later, Terri reached for her crutch and shuffled into the outdoor space at the back of the cottage she shared with Michael. Cheyenne the collie followed.

'Good girl,' said Terri, giving her a pat on the head. It had been months since she'd been able to take her for a long walk; since the surgery Michael had been taking her out. Her recovery had been slow and difficult, the first tentative steps she'd taken had drained all the energy out of her body. But bit by bit she was regaining strength.

She eased herself into a wicker seat in the corner, by a painting of bright blue flowers and her fern plant. This was her chill-out space, where she tried to focus on the present, to stop her mind from racing. Today, though, it was harder. Her mind wandered with thoughts of Niall, as it did more often these days since lockdown had stripped her calendar of activities and separated her from her children and grandchildren. She focused on her breathing, on the sun on her face, on the greens and oranges and reds of her tomato plants, getting riper by the day.

How do you grieve someone who is still alive? she wondered. Sometimes if she watched the news or documentaries about children who had been missing for a long time, she'd recognise, in the eyes of the parents, a pain she shared. There was no resolution, no closure. She could cope and she could learn to accept but she would never fully heal.

She sat for a few moments before reaching for a pen and paper. Afterwards she would put a letter in the special box stored safely in a drawer, in the hope, however distant, that Niall might one day read it.

To My First-Born,

I have written you many letters since I first found out you were alive. It took nearly twenty-two years for them to give me any information about you. I hope this letter finds you healthy and happy. I know you have no concept of how we shared my body for nine months ... It felt so real, it felt so strange, just to know I was one day going to give life to a tiny new person — you.

My first encounter with motherhood was harsh, cold, and cruel too ... But nothing could prepare me for when I first saw your tiny little face. You gave me the most precious gift I have ever received, the meaning of unconditional love. I was eighteen with no real insight into what motherhood entailed. I learned through you, I felt as though I was floating above myself, in the warmest glow of pure love. I could not take my eyes away from you, and still recall your little hand, how it grasped my tiny finger like you knew my smell, my touch, my voice.

Sadly, I was not able to stand up to the people who had already decided your fate and mine. My state declared me an unfit mother; not permitted to mother you in your journey of life. To be the one you ran to, who would pick you up and hug you, stroke your face when you felt unwell. Rock you in my arms when you needed my warmth.

We were denied it all, even all the arguments we could have had, our different perspectives, our own interpretation of life itself … I hope you learned to explore your own world; find your own view, your own path, what I would have given to have crossed your path with your permission even once.

In the short few weeks, they allowed me access to you at feeding times, I delayed this every time, as every second with you was all I had; to keep our memories alive for both of us. I hope my genes flow within you. I hope my love of music flows inside of you; above all I hope you are the man you were born to be. A man of integrity, love, with a free will to truly make your own real choices …

I am a stranger to you, but you are not to me. Nor will you ever be. I am your mother and will be till my last breath is taken. They stole you away, but they could not take my love, my memory of you, my first-born, nor the piece of my heart that belongs to only you …

My love, from a distance I can wrap my arms around you, in the hope one day you will feel my energy embrace and mind you …

All my love,
Your mother,
Terri

Part Three

Deirdre's Story

Chapter Thirty-Seven

DUBLIN, 1981

Deirdre was surprised at how convincing she could be. All of the drama training she had done as a girl, all the reciting poems and putting on bits of plays in the arts centre with her friends, it was all coming in handy. That morning she'd bumped into a girl she knew from teacher training college; they'd exchanged the usual how are yous, and the other girl had asked her where she had been last term. Deirdre had switched into the pre-prepared script without even having to think.

'I was staying with friends of the family in Cork having some tests done. I'm OK now. We didn't really get to the bottom of anything,' she had said.

It was a carefully crafted story: specific enough to satisfy people's curiosity, but just vague enough not to encourage any further questions. And Deirdre was so well-cast in the role of a carefree, well-adjusted final-year teaching student that she could utter those lines without letting a flicker of emotion show on her face, sometimes even smiling.

'Glad to hear you're better,' the girl had said, before moving along with her day.

If she had probed a little deeper, Deirdre might have disclosed that, since the summer, her mind wasn't the same; everything had become a little blurred around the edges and she saw the world reflected back at her in a different, bleaker pattern. Perhaps, if they had talked a little more, she might have told her about a loneliness, a longing that ached, and she didn't know whether it would ever leave her.

Chapter Thirty-Eight

WEXFORD, 1980

Deirdre was in a slow, frustrating battle with the clock. She had been looking up at it all morning, but its hands barely budged around the clock face, stubbornly drawing out the last hour of her Saturday shift at the credit union. It wasn't that she minded the job; the £10 a day was enough to tide her over for the summer and her colleagues were people she knew from the town all her life. But on a hot Saturday in June, her mind felt like soup, and the last thing she felt like doing was filling in the account books, counting the coins, putting them in bank bags and balancing the till. She looked up again. It was one o'clock, thank God. She grabbed her bag, relieved to escape the stuffy offices in Wexford Town.

On the way home, she passed the quay; people were making the most of the unexpectedly warm midsummer day, wandering around in the cotton dresses and shorts unworn since the year before, the children struggling to eat dripping ice-creams. She hadn't minded being back in Wexford for the holidays as much as she thought; college, she had to admit, was a bit of a disappointment. She'd longed to study French at Trinity – she'd imagined herself discussing books in other languages, taking part in debates, planning language exchanges abroad with her classmates. But when her parents had sat her down in her final year of school and explained the reality of their financial situation, she'd accepted that a subsidised place in teacher training college was as good as it was going to get. 'We can't afford to pay the fees for UCD or Trinity,' they had told her. Teaching was three years of lower fees, which would give her a guaranteed good job and a pension.

Instead of the lofty lecture halls of her imagination, Deirdre had found herself sitting around a small table while a middle-aged nun taught her and the other students the primary school curriculum as if they themselves were in junior infants. There were few guys there; the college had only recently started accepting male students. And she couldn't even skip lectures. Once when she'd been slightly the worse for wear after a party and stayed in the common room, her coat wrapped around her like a duvet, the nun had sent one of the other girls to get her.

It got to her a little bit, being such a dutiful daughter all the time. Things weren't looking good for the Bob Marley concert in Dalymount Park either. The tickets were seven pounds and she could just about afford it. But it wasn't like she could call in sick; her mother, Mary, worked in the credit union on a Saturday too and her father, Luke, was on the board. 'Saturday is the busiest day,' Luke had reminded her when she'd inquired about a day off. As she made the rest of the short journey to the family's semi-detached house on the outskirts of the town, she thought of the house party some guys she knew were hosting, and she hoped it would help her take her mind off things.

When she got there, people were already milling around, drinking beers and listening to Depeche Mode. Deirdre had taken extra care getting ready, choosing her long skirt and cheesecloth top. She looked around for Patrick* in the crowd – she had been hanging out with him in a big group down at the quay; he was a skinny guy, handsome in his own angular way. When they'd first been introduced, Deirdre had got that nervous, fizzy feeling you get when you fancy someone new.

As she danced and gossiped at the party with her friends about who would shift who, she got the impression Patrick's eyes were on her. At the end of the night she'd found herself opposite him, then kissing him.

'I guess I'll see you around,' he told her.

If Deirdre had anything to do with it, he definitely would.

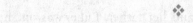

After a couple more meetings at parties, they started officially going out, seeing each other during the daytime. He drank and smoked too much, but it was the summer; she'd let that go. For a while she was intrigued – he was sensitive and had a brooding quality about him that she liked. He had some family problems and had left school early to work in a factory. It was handy that he had his own place, a tiny bedsit in the town attached to a B&B. It was their own space where they could come and drink a few beers, smoke weed and listen to Neil Young and James Taylor.

She didn't have the same fear with Patrick as she'd had with her previous boyfriend. They had gone out for a year and a half and Deirdre had been afraid of going too far. Sex was for when you got married: that was what she'd learned in school – probably the only mention of sex she'd heard in the classroom apart from the scratchy tapes they'd all giggle at when the nuns had played them on the tape recorder. But now that she was eighteen, surrounded by college friends and new ideas, she felt ready for a bit of rebellion. Sex was natural, she thought. Why shouldn't she enjoy it?

'This is amazing,' Deirdre told Patrick as she tasted the meal of spiced chickpeas and rice handed out by the group of Hare Krishnas who had set up a stall at Carnsore Point. 'And free as well.'

They were both starving after their swim, glad to take a moment to sit outside their wobbly tent on a blanket. They'd been at the anti-nuclear rally since the previous afternoon; Deirdre had been determined not to miss out on the second big event of the summer. Though it was a political gathering, it had the feel of a music festival; Christy Moore roused the crowd with 'Hiroshima, Nagasaki, Russian Roulette'. When the events wound up in the evening, they'd go to a friend's tent to hear some more music.

Patrick wasn't into the political speeches in the debate tents as much as she was, but it didn't matter; she was falling in love with the festival atmosphere, the idea of a common environmental cause.

Chapter Thirty-Nine

WEXFORD, 1981

Whore. Prostitute. Sinner.

Deirdre's own mother had called her those awful names; she'd never heard Mary use language like that. In her bedroom, her thoughts raced.

Earlier on that grey January morning she had put on her faux-fur astrakhan coat and set off for the doctor's. Over the past couple of months she had lost some weight and had felt nauseous. She hadn't paid any attention to it, busy with assignments and exams and single life in Dublin; she and Patrick had broken up when she'd gone back to college.

Mary, a bit concerned, had rung the doctor when Deirdre had come home for the weekend; the doctor advised Deirdre to come in and see him.

'Well, if you think we should,' Deirdre had said when he'd suggested a pregnancy test. 'But I don't think it's that.'

It was that. She was about four months in. Sheepish, she slinked out of the surgery.

On the short walk back past the Woolworths and the small grocery shops, Deirdre tried to get her head around it. It could have been a lot worse, she thought, there could have been something seriously wrong with her. She'd have a baby, and she'd get on with it. Her parents would get used to the idea. Walking up the path, she braced herself for their reaction.

She hadn't got past the hall before her mother called out to her.

'Well, how was it?'

'I'm pregnant.' There. She'd said it out loud.

Listening to the string of insults, she'd wondered if her mother might have preferred if she'd told her she had cancer.

Back in the bedroom, she shivered, pulling the covers around her. She had been her mother's cherished child, conceived after years of trying. Her parents were older than her friends' parents; her father worked all the hours he could in the post office to pay school fees for Deirdre and her younger sister. And her mother made every penny stretch as far as it could so that the girls could be in the same class as the daughters of doctors and solicitors, have the choices they couldn't otherwise have. Deirdre was the academic one, the girl who learned to read from a really young age; her mother had read all her stories and poems and school reports, proud of the bright shining star who would have a stable job and a third-level qualification. This new coldness unsettled Deirdre, the feeling of being knocked from a pedestal.

'What if I kept the baby?' she asked.

'Where would you live?' her mother replied. 'You'll have to go into digs where someone can keep an eye on you. I want you home here every weekend. And you can't tell your sister or anyone else about this. Especially not Patrick.'

'It's a moral problem,' her mother said to someone on the phone a few weeks later. She still had that stern, businesslike tone in her voice. Every weekend that Deirdre had come home from college she had hoped for a thaw in relations, that her mother would have softened, forgiven her. But she spoke to her with the same frostiness, barely meeting her eyes when she addressed her. And her father kept out of it, leaving her mother to deal with the women's business.

'I'd like to speak to the mother superior, please,' Mary said. Deirdre guessed it was a phone call to the Sisters of Charity. Her aunt was part of the congregation but her mother had gone straight to her superior. She didn't hear much more of the conversation but she knew it was about her. It was horrible, being a 'moral problem'. She felt dirty and ashamed.

Deirdre struggled to read the Agatha Christie book she had been trying to distract herself with. Normally she could lose herself trying to pick out all of the author's deftly laid clues, the murder mysteries that could be neatly solved with Poirot's help. But she couldn't focus; it was as if all the air in the house had become stale and heavy, there was no part of it untouched by this new atmosphere. She heard the phone click as her mother hung up.

'There is a place you can go until all this is over,' said her mother as she opened the door. 'It might be for the best.'

Deirdre nodded. Maybe it would be the best thing for all of them. Maybe then she'd get her mother back too – the clever, funny, vibrant woman she hadn't laughed with in ages, who looked at her daughter like she was a stranger.

In April, Deirdre packed her jeans and her loose shirts and jumpers into a bag. Three nuns greeted her at the door: Sister Justine, Sister Mary and Sister Martha.

The hall smelled faintly of furniture polish and Sister Justine led her down the corridor to a small reception room. Deirdre's mind wandered, dipping in and out as Sister Justine was speaking.

'It's best not to reveal too much about your home life, to keep things private. Lots of girls pick a new name to help with that. You can pick your own if you want,' she said.

Deirdre nodded. 'I guess Ciara might be alright? It sounds a bit like Deirdre.'

Sister Mary, a small woman in her fifties, led her up a big wooden staircase to the girls' quarters. The room was sparsely decorated, with two single beds and a wardrobe. Deirdre hoped the other girl would be nice. Everything had been so serious lately.

'Ciara, I'll leave you to it. Some of the girls have a chip on their shoulder, but you, you have nuns in the family, so you understand,' Sister Mary said, closing the door and leaving Deirdre on her own.

Deirdre wasn't sure she understood anything; for the past couple of months nothing had felt in her control. It's just a few months, she told herself. Soon all this would be over and she could start getting her life back ...

Chapter Forty

BESSBOROUGH, 1981

Deirdre took out her books, the Maria Montessori and Paulo Freire texts she had brought with her. Even though she was about to have a baby, her exams still loomed over her. Sister Regina from her training college had been kind when she'd told her. 'You won't be the first girl this happens to, and you won't be the last,' she had said. Then it was settled, Deirdre could take the repeat exams in August and be back in Carysfort in September as normal. That was the plan anyway.

She turned up the Superser. It was May but the downstairs room she shared with Orla, another education student, was cold and didn't get much light, and it meant that she had to put up with the gas smell mingling with the smell of the day's lunch which had wafted downstairs from the kitchen. Stew, she guessed. Again. Settling back into her book, she realised she had read the same page twice, not taking in any of the information. The theory of education would have to wait another day, she thought, closing the book.

From her notebook she pulled out one of the letters she had received. Writing to people felt more like fiction-writing these days; she had done as her parents had said and hadn't confided in anyone, her loose clothes hiding the bump on her slim frame. There was a system in Bessborough: the outgoing letters were sent to the addresses of local families and forwarded from there, so that no one would figure out the girls were in a convent. Deirdre still hadn't replied to one of her friends back in Wexford who had been asking about her, wondering when Deirdre would be back from having the tests in hospital. Deirdre responded to the question but kept it vague. 'Thanks for thinking of me,' she wrote. 'I'm looking forward to getting back home.' That much was honest at least. But there were so many half-truths, so many secrets. She hadn't had a proper conversation with anyone in months and it felt so lonely.

After lunch, Deirdre made her way to the nursery, to report for duty. The study exemption was only for weekday mornings; in the afternoons and at the weekends she was expected to join the other girls at work. The nursery was a large space with the same pale-coloured walls and dark wood, the rows of cots arranged at each end of the room. Deirdre knew what to do: she made up a bottle and picked up a gorgeous, chubby little girl a few months old, sitting her down on her knee. The baby took it hungrily, and Deirdre could see her little chest rise and fall with each breath. The radio hummed in the background, but Deirdre could barely hear it over the chatter of the other girls and the occasional shrieks of the babies.

These afternoons in the nursery were always the hardest part of her day. It wasn't the work – the babies were adorable and she had got used to the smell of sour nappies and baby formula. But as she held the baby close, seeing her trying to reach for things with her little arms, she couldn't help thinking about the baby's mother, the girl who had been in the nursery with them a few weeks ago. Soon Deirdre would leave after she gave birth to her own baby. She would be back in Wexford, while someone else fed, washed and dressed her child. Stop, she told herself, forcing her mind to focus on other things. What good would it do?

The baby drifted back to sleep after finishing the bottle. Deirdre sat with her for a while, then set her back down in the cot and made her way slowly to the door. On her way, she passed Maria, the youngest girl in the home, with long fair hair and a round, childlike face. She was only about thirteen or fourteen and every time Deirdre saw her she felt a stab of pity, imagining how lonely she must feel. She rarely spoke to anyone, and the bump looked so out of place on her small body. When she had first arrived, Deirdre had shared a room with her for a couple of days before a single bedroom became available opposite Orla. Maria sobbed every night for her mother and there was nothing Deirdre or anyone else could say to comfort her.

The in-house chapel was an airy room on the ground floor, not far from the nursery. Lately, Deirdre had been spending more and more time there, to reflect and to escape from the noise. The faint smell of incense reminded her of mass in her local church as a child; the atmosphere was comforting, quiet and familiar. As a child, she had been fascinated by the idea of joining a convent, the certainty of a vocation; she'd been in awe of a fierce nun in the primary school she'd been to, who didn't seem to care what anybody else thought. Then there was the drama of all the stories they read about in religion class – to Deirdre, they were almost like ghost stories, with their visions and apparitions that could happen at any moment. As she became a teenager, the idea had lost its shine, but she could sometimes still see the appeal. She went to mass once a week, still said her prayers, still believed, in her own way.

In a small room behind the chapel, the local priest gestured for Deirdre to take a seat. 'Bless me, Father, for I have sinned,' she began. 'It has been six months since my last confession.' She poured it all out, asked for God's forgiveness that she had disappointed her parents, had let them down, had had sex outside marriage without thinking of the consequences. Now she was paying for her 'mistake', as the nuns liked to call it, and she would do anything she could to make it up to everybody.

'Did you enjoy it?' he asked her.

Deirdre was honest. 'Yes.'

'Well, then, my advice to you is find a nice boy and marry him as quickly as possible.'

Chapter Forty-One

BESSBOROUGH, 1981

'Is there nothing they can do to speed things up?' Luke asked.

Deirdre had lumbered her way down the big wooden staircase to take the call. She was about eight and a half months pregnant, sleeping little and generally feeling exhausted. She wasn't looking forward to heading back up those stairs again.

These conversations were always strained. On the phone, her father's voice was tense. She was worried about him, about both of her parents. When they'd come to visit and take her out for tea in a coffee shop in Cork City, they hadn't looked well. Luke's angina was flaring up, making him more susceptible to a heart attack, and Mary was pale and brittle; she had had a bout of colitis. It was so different from all of the other visits they'd made to Cork, to go to see her mother's people in the old farmhouse; Deirdre had loved the trips to the bog with her uncle, the stark landscape and the lambs and the calves. Her mother had seemed so happy on those visits and Deirdre had always associated Cork with that, the freedom of running around a farm, the family relaxed in each other's company, not the grinding days in a grey building and the awkward silences that were her reality now.

'Ever since this happened, we're trying to keep the secrets up,' Luke told her.

'I'll ask the sister,' Deirdre told him, hanging up. Maybe there was something that could be done.

The hospital part of the home was downstairs, along a corridor through a door on the left, which led onto more modern rooms. All of the maternity care was done in-house, and the home was equipped with a labour ward and a delivery room. Deirdre knocked on the door of the small office.

'Ciara. Come in. How are things? Must be near the end for you now.'

It surprised her, how quickly she had got used to having a different name. Deirdre had learned to respond without even pausing for a second.

'My parents are worried. My mother's not well. I'd like to get home soon, if I can.'

'Well, we'll examine you then, shall we?'

In the check-up room, Deirdre eased herself onto the table.

'Well, the head is engaged. We can induce you next week.'

Deirdre nodded. Anything that got her home sooner was the right thing to do.

❖

'Good luck,' said Orla.

The other girl squeezed Deirdre's hand before she was ushered out of the delivery room by the matron and her assistant. Hooked up to a drip, Deirdre lay on a metal trolley, looking at the cool white walls, the frosted glass of the delivery room. Within a couple of hours she was floored by the pain, which came in excruciating waves. Her pregnancy book hadn't prepared her for this; the contractions overpowered her and they went on for hours. She was alone, apart from the occasional visits from the matron or the assistant to see how she was doing, and she wished it to be over. Later she passed out, perhaps from an analgesic.

When she woke up, she wondered how she had ended up on the other side of the room. She could see the assistant.

'Is it going to be much longer?' she asked her.

'Don't worry. Your mother's been on the phone.'

'But will it be much longer?'

'Oh, you've had your child. You have a baby boy.'

Deirdre fell into another deep sleep. She woke up the following morning in the home's small maternity ward, a room at the end of the corridor with six beds. She moved to get up but flinched with the pain, her body giving her a sign that she needed to stay still.

'Don't get up,' the matron told her. 'You haemorrhaged and you need to rest. It was a forceps delivery. We had to give you an episiotomy and you've had a lot of stitches.'

Deirdre stayed in bed for the next three days, woozy from the pain and the medication. She felt well enough to move on her birthday, 19 June, and she shuffled her way to the nursery to see her son. She took him in her arms, overcome by the love she felt for him. She couldn't take her eyes off him: a healthy baby with her colouring, the very dark hair, almost black. He had a long, sturdy body, was making little sounds and sighs. She called him Paul. She'd heard stories about grandparents having a change of heart as soon as the baby arrived; once they saw Paul, how could her parents possibly leave him behind? She could take a year out from Carysfort until she got settled, and she'd work it out.

A couple of hours later, the matron told her to gather her things; her parents had come to pick her up.

'Come and take a look at him,' said Deirdre, guiding them

into the nursery, past the rows of cots, until she stopped in front of his.

Luke smiled. 'He's a grand little fella,' he said, peering into the cot. Mary said nothing, her face inscrutable. Deirdre felt her body tense with anxiety. After a few minutes, they turned to go and Deirdre knew it was over, her eyes filling with hot tears. One of the nuns led her into a small room to sign the first set of papers.

She walked into the courtyard to say goodbye to the other girls, Orla giving her a brief hug before pressing a folded-up note into Deirdre's hand. Deirdre knew she'd probably never see her or hear from her again; she didn't even know her real name to look her up in the phone book. As the car pulled away, she unfolded the note, crumpled now and wet with tears.

'A brave soldier never looks back,' it read, in Orla's swirly, joined-up handwriting. She'd drawn a smiley face at the bottom of it.

She was right, Deirdre thought. Paul was staying behind in the home and she wouldn't be able to get him back. The only thing she could do now was to try to put everything out of her mind. She had to drop the cloak of Ciara and go back to being Deirdre, a bright girl training to be a teacher. But she never imagined it would be so hard.

Bessborough 1980–99

I first met Deirdre in the outdoor area of a Dublin coffee shop. I saw her approach in a bright red coat with a hint of purple and the first thing that struck me was how young she looked, perhaps the same age as one of my aunts; her first son, born in Bessborough, is the same age as my older sister. When I pointed this out to her, how recent it seemed for her to have been admitted to a mother and baby institution, she nodded, as if it was a question that she was very familiar with. 'It was a very, very different country ... but it's not that long ago,' she told me. 'I met a young man at a community gathering and he had been born in Bessborough in 1991, so his mother was there ten years after me.'

Deirdre was a natural storyteller; she was very descriptive and her lifelong love of poetry meant she sometimes spoke in figurative language. She saw it as a sort of personal duty to use those gifts to speak out about her experiences. 'If there is something I can do, it is to be open, to encourage other people to empower themselves to speak and to break that silence and secrecy as well,' she told me. Sometimes our conversations veered off into other things she was very passionate about: the housing crisis, the far-right and misinformation online. After that first meeting in Dublin, I visited her in her small cottage in rural Wexford, and when we spoke on the phone, I imagined her sitting in the snug by the fire, wearing a long, flowing dress, a modern-day feminist *seanchaí*. There are small parts of her experiences she found hard to remember. 'It's so weird, you'd think these things would be etched on your brain, but I think with trauma very often there's a lot of blurring of details,' she explained.

Looking through the information I could access, I could see that in 1981, the year Deirdre was in her second year of college and entered Bessborough, admissions to mother and baby homes were still high. Throughout the 1980s, almost 1,500 women and girls passed through Bessborough's doors, and the average stay for women and girls was less than three months. For children, it was about six to seven weeks.[19] In the early years of the decade, most children born there were placed for adoption. Though basic supports were available, such as the unmarried mother's allowance and statutory maternity leave, introduced in 1981, Deirdre said she was never made aware of alternatives to adoption. 'That was never put to me and I doubt it was put to any of the other girls ... Nobody said you could keep your child and have support if you don't have support from home.'

An internal report published by the congregation of the Sisters of the Sacred Hearts of Jesus and Mary in 1982 described 'a comprehensive programme' offered to women and girls admitted to the institution. This included 'medical and obstetrical care; child care; individual/group counselling; group living; continuation of school education; adoptions; fostering; post-adoption family counselling and help with extra-marital pregnancies'. The aim of the programme, according to the report, was 'to help the girl accept the new life within her. We do this by helping her understand her situation, to restore her feelings of self-worth and esteem. At the same time, we are acutely conscious of the pressures on the single pregnant girl'.[20]

Some of these pressures may have referred to the attitudes towards unmarried mothers, which remained deeply hostile in the early 1980s. The same year that the internal report was circulated, Eileen Flynn, a secondary school teacher in a convent school in Wexford, was dismissed when she became pregnant while living with a married man. The Employment Appeals Tribunal upheld the right of the religious order to dismiss her from her role because of her lifestyle. When Ms Flynn appealed this judgement to the High Court, the court ruled that the decision did not constitute unfair dismissal. Two years later, in 1984, a fifteen-year-old schoolgirl called Ann Lovett was found dead near a Marian grotto in Granard, County Longford. She had died giving birth and had told no one about the pregnancy. Deirdre remembers this time clearly, a time when she could empathise with other women but not show any compassion for herself. 'I could look at Ann Lovett and Granard and what happened there and go, "Oh my God, that's horrendous," but I didn't think what had happened to me was horrendous. I thought it was my fault.' And in 1983, two years after Deirdre left Bessborough, Irish people voted to introduce the eighth amendment to the constitution. This gave an equal right to life to the mother and to the unborn, effectively banning abortion.

As the decade progressed, things started to change in the Bessborough home. But by the mid-1980s the numbers of women and girls admitted had started to decline and more were deciding to keep their babies. With numbers falling, Bessborough started to cater for specific groups: students, women and girls with special needs, women and girls on their second pregnancy, and women and girls with difficult family circumstances, and so on. Those admitted could take vocational education courses in hairdressing, typing or electronics.

In 1985, the Sisters of the Sacred Hearts of Jesus and Mary agreed to discontinue maternity services in the home to bring services in line with those provided to other women around the country, as the maternity hospital in Bessborough was not staffed by a consultant. Mother and baby institutions should have 'a social function only',[21] according to a Department of Health letter written at the time. That same year, contraception became available without prescription, allowing young women to make choices about their sexual lives.

By 1986, conversations were already taking place in the Department of Health about closing mother and baby homes. The department said that 'greater tolerance and compassion'[22] towards single mothers, along with the introduction of the unmarried mother's allowance and the increasing numbers of women going to the UK to seek an abortion, had led to a smaller number of admissions in mother and baby homes. A year later, the legal concept of 'illegitimacy' was abolished under the Status of Children Act, 1987.

From 1986 to 1992, 826 women, or an average of 118 women a year, were admitted to Bessborough. By 1998 this had dropped to thirty-seven admissions a year. In July 1998, the congregation wrote to the Irish Adoption Board to say that they had decided to withdraw from the placement of babies for adoption.[23] The congregation said that it wished to focus on 'the care of expectant women' and on 'search and reunion'. That same year, a case decided in the Supreme Court, I. O'T vs B, would complicate the situation for adopted people searching for their natural relatives. The case involved two women adopted informally before the practice became legal in Ireland in 1953. They wished for the institution that had placed them with families as children to release the identity of their natural mothers. In a complex ruling, the Supreme Court found that the right to privacy for natural mothers outweighed the right to information for adopted people. That decision affected subsequent attempts to bring in adoption and tracing legislation, with successive Attorneys General advising against granting identity rights to adopted people.[24]

One year later, in November 1999, the last woman and child were discharged from Bessborough and it ceased to operate as a mother and baby institution. By then, Paul had turned eighteen, and Deirdre was embarking on a search to trace him. In the intervening years, the impact of that loss would complicate her life, relationships and mental health in a myriad of different ways.

Chapter Forty-Two

WEXFORD, 1981

10th September 1981

My dear Deirdre,
I hope these few lines will find you well and not studying too
hard. I enclose the photo of Paul for you. I think he is lovely
and his parents are absolutely thrilled with him. They called
him Mark*. He is lovely and dark and very like his new father.
He has been as good as gold and never gave them the slightest
trouble. He is very healthy, thank God. I was hoping to have
had the photograph before you returned to college, but I am sure
your parents will send it on. I do hope you will do well in your
exams, Deirdre. God bless and good luck and anytime you want

news of Paul, just drop a note. They are going to adopt a little
girl next so he will have a little sister.
Love from all here,
Yours affectionately,
Sister Justine

It was a single, handwritten page, but to Deirdre, desperate
for any bit of news, it was a lifeline. She read it again and
again upstairs in her bedroom since she had come back to
Wexford for the weekend from Dublin. The letter reiterated
what she had been told – that they were a lovely family;
she was so glad for Paul that he was being looked after by
good people, a couple who could give him all the things she
couldn't. But none of it made her miss him any less.

She took out the photo from the envelope. She was
really glad of it; her visual memories of Paul had become
more blurred in her mind as the weeks passed and she was
worried she'd forget what he looked like. She had tried to
picture him at one month, six months, twelve months, but
her recollections had come up short. Now she could see how
much he'd grown: he was round and sturdy, dressed in a
red babygro and white socks, perched on a white sheepskin
rug against a blue-grey background. He looked like a happy
little boy, she had to admit. By now he would have learned
to roll and hold his head up, some of the things she had
seen the babies do in the Bessborough nursery, and her eyes

stung with tears when she thought about all the things she'd never see.

She thought things would have got easier by now, she really did. She'd signed the second set of papers before she started college. At a party she'd told Patrick what had happened and he had understood. By some miracle, she had passed her exams and had gone back into digs in Dublin under the watchful eye of a landlady. Monday to Friday she shared a small room with two single beds with a friend from Wexford, and at the weekends she went home. Her health was better now after that spell in Cork, she told everyone. She was fine. But even in the city there were so many reminders, so many little things that started her off in a spiral of daydreams about Paul. She saw small children everywhere and her mind wandered when she saw a dark-haired baby in the street. Did he have brown eyes, her nose, her mouth? Was there any chance, however small, that it would be him?

Last week, in the college TV common room, she had struggled with a nappy ad. It was shot near a window with lots of light, featuring a photogenic toddler waddling around. And the images had entered her head. *A row of cots, a set of stone steps, a car door slamming shut.* And Deirdre willed her expression to remain the same, willed her mind to focus back on the TV in the corner. But it was too late. She'd seen it again. *A row of cots, a set of stone steps, the sound of a car door closing.* Flashes and fragments of her time in

Bessborough that reappeared no matter how hard she tried to banish them from her mind.

From the sitting room downstairs, Deirdre could hear the news on the TV. The headlines were all about the IRA hunger strikers these days; their names were daubed on the wall at Sunnybank corner in Bray where she and others stood to hitch a lift to Wexford. She took a breath, a few moments of stillness before she tidied away the letter and went in.

'Cup of coffee?' said Mary. If she'd looked at the envelope and seen that the letter she'd put on Deirdre's bed upstairs had come from Bessborough, she didn't mention it.

Deirdre nodded, settling herself into the chair as the brass band announced the start of *The Late Late Show*. She never used to mind staying in with her mother on a Saturday evening if she didn't have plans with her mates, the two of them seeing in the start of the weekend together in companionable silence while her father was at one of his credit union meetings. Now, three months after she'd come back from Bessborough, she was starting to think that the awkwardness wouldn't go away, that the gap between them might never be bridged. She laughed along with the studio audience, she nodded along to the interviews with newsmakers, the live music, the chat with the guests, the prize draws. Could Mary tell it was forced? she wondered.

When she'd first come back from Bessborough, she'd

been less good at pretending. She'd sobbed into her pillow at night. 'How can you possibly miss him?' her mother had asked her then. 'You only knew him for three days. I lost my brother when I was fifty-one.' And now when Deirdre felt like crying to herself in her room, she thought about the lengths to which her parents had gone to keep it hush-hush, how the nuns in Carysfort had kept everything a secret, how she had disappointed everyone and things were only just starting to go back to normal. The one thing she had to do was forget about it.

The host ended the show and the credits rolled. 'Goodnight,' Deirdre said to her mother as she made her way to bed. She was bone-weary all the time these days.

But there was another niggling thought that she couldn't share with anybody; she tried not to let her mind focus on it but it remained there regardless. The only thing that would make her feel better was another baby. One she could hold, cuddle and spoil. That was the only way she could ever get over losing Paul like that. The thought consumed her, and it took all the effort she could muster not to give into it; she didn't know what to do about that.

Chapter Forty-Three

DUNBOYNE, 1982

'Deirdre, whatever you do, don't tell any of the other girls that it's your second time,' Sister Claire had warned her when she arrived.

Deirdre's cheeks burned. She didn't need to ask why. She was twenty, a newly qualified primary teacher from a good family, someone people were supposed to look up to. Having two children she couldn't keep wasn't a good look for a young *múinteoir*.

It was all getting very close now: in a few short weeks, her second baby would be born. As Deirdre had taken the taxi to the imposing Georgian house on a sprawling patch of land in County Meath, she noticed how similar the Dunboyne mother and baby institution was to Bessborough: it too was built on acres of lush countryside; it too had a confusing mix of original period features and an out-of-place newer section. There were designated areas for the girls: shared bedrooms, communal bathrooms, a TV room, a dining room and a visitors' room. To her, it seemed grimmer somehow, with less light, though perhaps that was also down to the time of year, the end of autumn, a crisp chill turning to the damp, soggy cold of an Irish winter.

'In Dunboyne all the girls go to Holles Street for their maternity care,' another nun told her. 'We don't do it in-house here. One of us drives the minibus there every week for your check-ups.'

Listening to the nuns, the lack of maternity hospital seemed to be the only real difference; everything else they described, from the ethos to the routine to the house names, appeared to be exactly the same. Unpacking her things in the small room she shared with two other girls, Deirdre wondered how on earth she had managed to end up in one of these places again.

For a while at least, finding out she was pregnant again had given Deirdre a jolt, had brought her back down to reality and forced her to focus. In the months beforehand, she had continued to stumble through her life in a fog that blurred her senses. She'd had a boyfriend, Jack*, whom she met in Wexford at the weekends; he was a good listener and she'd ignored all the gossip about what he got up to during the week. Then in the spring, her period didn't arrive and she got the tell-tale nausea. I can't put my parents through this again, she told herself. This is all my fault, and I have to find a way out of this mess.

She put her head down for her final term of college and got through her exams. 'I'm sorry, I can't continue with this,' she told Jack when she went home to Wexford one weekend. As the term progressed, she went home less and less. In the summer, she worked with some friends who converted a post office telegraph van into a food truck, travelling to festivals and selling pancakes. In the phonebook she found a number for the Rotunda Girls Aid Society, a Catholic adoption society with offices in the Pro-Cathedral on Dublin's Marlborough Street. 'I can't go home to my parents,' she said when she went to visit in person, 'but I want to leave it as late as possible before I go into a mother and baby home.' The woman nodded, giving her a number of a mother and baby institution in Dunboyne, run by the Good Shepherd Sisters. Deirdre told everyone she'd found an au pair job in Meath, something to tide her over until she could get a teaching job; she had no idea whether they believed it. She didn't have the energy to care.

❖

In Dunboyne, Deirdre rooted around in her purse for some coins; she hadn't yet rung her mother. For the past month, she had called her every week from the home's payphone, making up stories about a non-existent family in Ashbourne with noisy, energetic little boys who took up all of her energy as an au pair. She'd given them the names John and Joseph, after the two girls she shared a room with whose house names were Joan and Josephine.

'Hello, Deirdre, how are you doing?' said Mary.

If only Deirdre could answer honestly. She wasn't grand, she wasn't doing well. She was going through the motions, trying not to draw attention to herself. She spent her mornings and afternoons packing and folding greeting cards into boxes in a prefab around the back of the house. She had some light cleaning duties, dusting and polishing the communal areas. In the evenings, she did a bit of knitting – one of the girls had started her off and she'd made two Icelandic fishing sweaters, one for her father as a present, the thick wool knitting up satisfyingly quickly. But no matter how vigorously she scrubbed or folded or clacked the knitting needles, she couldn't shake the desolate feeling she had from the moment she woke up in the morning until she fell asleep at night.

'I'm fine, how are you?' she asked Mary, trying her best to sound upbeat.

They went through the usual pleasantries, the updates Deirdre had from her fictional job hunt, inquiries after her health. Deirdre asked how her father and sister were doing. Mary's voice sounded a bit strange, as if there was something she wanted to say but couldn't bring herself to. The warning beep sounded to alert Deirdre that she was running out of money, but when she shook her purse, she couldn't find any more coins.

'I have to go, sorry, I'm running out of money.'

'But Deirdre—'

As she walked away from the phone, she heard it ring again and her heart sank. Her mother had been a telephonist before she got married; Deirdre knew she would have called the exchange to be reconnected with her.

'Is that you? Are you in trouble?'

'What do you mean?'

'I know where you are. When I rang the exchange they told me you were in the Good Shepherd Convent.'

There was no other option but to admit it, let it all out. 'I just wanted to protect you,' Deirdre told her. At least she didn't have to lie to her any more. In a way, it was a relief.

The Holles Street maternity ward was cramped and there was so little privacy. Thin curtains separated the beds and Deirdre could hear every bit of her neighbours' conversations, the cries and squeals of the other babies. There was a steady stream of other mothers waiting to give birth pacing up and down the sloped corridors. Deirdre couldn't have cared less. Her baby boy sighed and gurgled in the cot next to her bed; she traced her finger around his tiny mouth, his tufts of fair hair. This time she wanted to make the most of the time she had with her new baby on their own together. I'm still his mother, she thought, even if it's just for a short time. It wouldn't be fair to breastfeed, she reminded herself, though she wished she could.

It had been such an easy birth compared to the last time. Her waters had broken in the early hours of the morning and the nun on duty in Dunboyne called her a taxi to bring her to the hospital. The contractions came thick and fast, and her baby was born forty-five minutes after she arrived at Holles Street; she had only just been settled in the small, cramped labour ward before she had to push. There was no pethidine, no invasive procedures; she was much more in control. The day after, a friend she trusted from Dublin had visited her and brought her a new nightdress and some baby clothes.

Beside her, the baby startled slightly. Deirdre got such a kick out of watching his little gulps and yawns, his face scrunching up and relaxing. Diarmuid, she thought. That suits him. She'd always loved Irish names, had been fascinated by Irish myths and legends, the wild and fearless adventures of Diarmuid and Gráinne who ran off together, defying a powerful chief. She eased herself out of bed and phoned Mary from the hospital.

'It's a little boy. Diarmuid. He's so beautiful.'

Mary sighed.

'Maybe I can keep him this time?' she'd said, her voice weakening as she uttered the words.

'And how can you do that?' said her mother. 'What if your first son comes looking for you and finds out that you kept the second child? How is he going to feel?'

Deirdre shuffled back to bed, defeated. Mary was right.

How could she have thought her situation was like the woman in the bed next to her, cooing over her newborn, her partner sitting in a chair beside her, delighted with them both. How could she think she could be the same as her when the doctor who examined her carried out his duties without a word, or when one of the senior nurses scolded her for 'not knowing better', within earshot of all the other mothers.

'The taxi will be here soon, Deirdre.' One of the nurses popped her head around the curtain to tell her. She had known it was coming; she'd given birth three days ago and the doctor had given her a clean bill of health. She gathered her few things together, packed her red dressing gown into her bag, changed and dressed Diarmuid, drawing it out as long as she could, taking her time getting his little arms and legs into the babygro. She knew the score; babies rarely returned to Dunboyne and were cared for elsewhere before being given to adoptive parents.

Another Dunboyne girl met her at reception and the taxi drove out to St Patrick's on the Navan Road, a mother and baby institution run by the Daughters of Charity; it was a red-brick, five-storey building with neatly trimmed hedges and white-painted iron balconies. A couple of years ago she had known nothing about institutions like this; now she saw that they were dotted around everywhere. She walked around to the side door and knocked; one of the nuns answered and nodded at Deirdre. The nun took Diarmuid from her arms and Deirdre stood in the doorway, watching her walk away until the door banged shut.

Chapter Forty-Four

WEXFORD, 1983

'I haven't signed them yet,' Deirdre said. She had been back in Wexford for a couple of weeks but hadn't yet signed the adoption papers. Until she did, there was still a possibility, however small, that she could keep Diarmuid.

'How would you bring up a child?' said Mary. 'He'd be dragged up. A child needs to have a stable home and two parents,' she continued. 'You wouldn't be able to teach. You'd have to get some other job and be in some flat somewhere. It would be the most selfish thing in the world if you kept that child.'

Deirdre hated to admit it but it was true that no primary school would hire a single mother who wasn't married. No board of management would approve the appointment.

She looked at the clock; she would have to leave now if she was going to make the next bus from Wexford Town to Dublin. She grabbed her coat and bag and headed towards the door. At the bus stop, she waited, looked around to see if Jack had come, as he had said he would when she'd told him about Diarmuid and her weekly visits to St Patrick's. But like the week before and the week before that, he hadn't.

Passing a woman she knew as she made her way to her seat, Deirdre flashed a brief smile.

'Up shopping again, are you, Deirdre?' said the other woman.

Deirdre nodded and turned her head towards the window. Getting off on the Navan Road, she walked down the short path to the entrance she took to get to the nursery in St Pat's; it too was similar to Bessborough, with its painted iron cots. It was staffed by lay nursery nurses, whom she found kind – they chatted to her, asked about Diarmuid and occasionally took the odd photo.

Diarmuid wriggled in his cot; he was about five weeks old and becoming more alert every day. She picked him up, positioned him on her knee and rocked him until he was settled and content. Then she reached for her bag, taking out a stuffed baby koala she had bought for him; it had soft brown fur and brown buttons for eyes. She attached it to the baby's cot, wrapping its arms around the wooden bars; she'd ask the nurse to take a photo of Diarmuid when she got a chance; he was changing every day and she wanted to remember him as he was now. Probably the fairest thing I can do for this child is to let him be, to allow him to have a new life with a family who can provide for him, she thought. That was the right thing, wasn't it?

'I don't want him to be an only child,' Deirdre told the social worker. Her name was Maureen*, and she was perhaps in her thirties or forties – Deirdre couldn't really tell. She'd come back into Dublin for an appointment arranged by the Rotunda Girls Aid Society to discuss the plan for Diarmuid. The session was about discussing the profiles of prospective adoptive parents, to seek Deirdre's input as to who she felt would be the right match.

'This family looks suitable,' said Maureen as she sheafed through a bundle of papers. 'They live in north Dublin and both of the parents have big extended families. How do they sound to you?'

She passed Deirdre the file so she could read through it; as Deirdre flicked through the pages, she imagined her child running into kitchens filled with cousins and aunts and uncles, a noisy childhood in a home with lots of warmth.

'They sound like a good match.' It was a struggle to get the words out.

'How are you feeling about it all, Deirdre?'

Deirdre gathered herself. 'I'm fine, I mean physically I'm getting back to normal and Diarmuid is doing great. I go to visit him and he's being well looked after. We're both fine, really.'

'And how is the job hunt going? It says on your file that you're a teacher.'

'It's hard. There isn't much around at the moment. I apply for everything I see but it's the same for all of us; there's a lot of unemployment right now.'

'And how are things at home?'

'They're not great, but they're improving. It's a process, I suppose, it will take time.'

'You intellectualise everything, Deirdre. You're in your head. You don't talk about your feelings.'

Deirdre nodded in agreement, but Maureen didn't understand. If Deirdre talked about how she really felt, she would start crying and would struggle to stop; she wouldn't be able to have a normal conversation. She still didn't dare think about her feelings. She shut them away in a dark corner of her mind, fearful that if she let them take over, they would hold her in their grip and she wouldn't be able to carry on.

Adoption Board
65 Merrion Square
Dublin
19th October 1983

Dear Miss Wadding,
You will probably recall that when you were interviewed
last February in connection with your consent to the
adoption of the child Diarmuid you asked to be told the
date of the making of the adoption order for him. Accordingly,
I am to inform you that the Board proposes to make the
order on _____.

Yours sincerely,

_____

Chapter Forty-Five

WEXFORD, 1990

'Don't ever worry about your weight again,' Deirdre's mother told her as she sank back into the bath.

Deirdre nodded. Weight had been a constant battle for Mary – she'd been on a diet for as long as Deirdre could remember. But now she was skeletal, frail, her skin almost like paper. It didn't suit her.

A couple of months ago, a blip in a scan had led to surgery, then to a cancer at so late a stage it was untreatable. Her father and sister did what they could, but Deirdre had been the strong one who made the soup, who bathed her, who had come back from her teaching job in Dublin to be her full-time carer.

'Will you clear away my clothes when I'm gone?' her mother asked her. 'Your father will be too upset.'

And Deirdre nodded again. Of course she'd do it.

When her mother had had more energy, they'd talked about what happens after someone dies; Deirdre knew her mother's faith was a comfort to her. Deep down, Deirdre suspected Mary still viewed her with disappointment; Deirdre who no longer went to mass, Deirdre, who at twenty-eight had only recently got a divorce in the UK from her first husband, because it wasn't legal in Ireland. That nice boy, her mother still referred to him as. The marriage had lasted ten months.

Sometimes she felt guilty about all of the resentment curdling under the surface between herself and Mary, all of the things that had been left unsaid. How can you pretend nothing has changed since I had the children? Deirdre wanted to ask her. How can you not even ask me about how I feel? I got married to a kind, decent man but it wasn't right. And then after we got back from our honeymoon, I thought to myself, 'What have I done?' and the whole thing broke down after a few months because all I could think about was having Diarmuid and Paul back. And I still think about them, your grandchildren, all the time; I try so hard to distract myself but sometimes I can't.

Helping her out of the bath, she guided Mary into a clean nightdress. When she was safely back in the bed, Deirdre pulled the covers up around her.

'Goodnight,' she told her. And it struck her how many times her mother would have tucked her into bed at night, told her stories.

It was too late; her mother was too sick. No point going into all of that now.

Chapter Forty-Six

DUBLIN AND WEXFORD, 1993

Saoirse was a March baby. She arrived eleven days late, on International Women's Day, as the winter frosts receded and the daffodils and tulips brought small bursts of colour to Deirdre's little corner of Dublin. All through the pregnancy she had felt so good, so hopeful. She'd accepted the well-wishes, had worn her maternity clothes with pride. It was a home birth in the apartment in the city where she lived with her second husband, Graham*; she'd found a supportive midwife and her pregnancy was low risk. Deirdre had ignored the raised eyebrows and the questions about whether she was doing the best thing for the baby. Let people say what they want, she thought. I'm near a hospital and of course I'll go there if there's an emergency. This time she didn't want to be managed, instructed, regulated, organised, told what to do and what not to do. Graham understood; she'd told him everything about Paul and Diarmuid from the very start.

Looking at her little daughter's rumpled face, all wrapped up in blankets, Deirdre had never felt so happy, so excited. The doctor and midwife had said they were both perfectly healthy and there'd been no judgement, no loud comments, no rush to leave or sign papers, no nosy neighbours craning their necks in the Holles Street maternity ward. And when Saoirse latched on and Deirdre had fed her for the first time, she couldn't believe that she was really hers, her own baby to mother and rear. She and Graham, a fellow teacher she'd met on a training course, were a team, staring in awe at their little girl, who had made them a family.

And this time, people were so excited for her and the baby. In the weeks that followed, there were flowers and pink cards with 'congratulations on your new baby girl' on them and gifts of soft toys and babygros and tiny jackets. There were so many people welcoming Saoirse into the world, celebrating her arrival. Deirdre couldn't help but compare it to the other times, when there had been no cards or gifts, when her mother had told her she was selfish to want to rear her child.

Graham clicked the camera as often as he could and Deirdre was always ready to flash a smile. She wanted to remember everything – the teething, the first steps, the birthday parties. Everything she had missed with Paul and Diarmuid, she would be there for all of it with Saoirse.

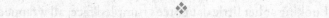

A few months later, Deirdre woke up feeling jittery. It's nothing, she told herself, just tiredness from the night feeds and the new mother's exhaustion kicking in. 'I'm fine,' she assured her husband, waving him off to work. 'We'll see you soon.' She felt the pulse racing in the palms of her hands as she reached for her cup of tea. She looked at Saoirse wriggling away on her blanket, checked her. Did she need another feed? No. To be changed? No. Did she have a fever? No. Was she sure? She checked again. Her hands shook slightly, and she felt sweaty. She sat down. Was she imagining it or did she feel dizzy? Stop it, she told herself. You've a baby to look after; you've loads to do. But how would she know if something was wrong? Saoirse is fine, she told herself, this is all in your head, more of these strange feelings you get sometimes.

Saoirse's grandfather was making silly faces at her, provoking squeals of laughter. Deirdre loved seeing them together; she felt closer to her dad than she had in a long time. She and Graham were staying with him while they were looking for a new house in Wexford. Deirdre suspected he welcomed the company. Mary's death three years ago had hit him hard. They'd had long chats, she and her dad, about what had happened in Bessborough, the years of silences. 'We didn't handle it all that well,' he'd admitted to her. And she'd talked it through with her younger sister, who had never been told. Sometimes, Deirdre wished her mother had been around to meet Saoirse; maybe she would have asked her about what was normal for babies that age, about all of the doubts she had about looking after her daughter that niggled at the back of her mind.

'You're miles away,' Graham said. Over dinner, she tried to put her worries out of her head, to listen to his stories of school, boisterous kids and upcoming visits from the inspector. She knew she didn't want to go back to teaching: the routine, a fixed timetable, that feeling of being tied to an ethos, a rigid system, when she could be at home with her daughter. She'd resigned from her permanent job with no regrets. 'I'm just tired,' she replied. 'Nothing a bit of sleep won't sort out.'

That night, she woke up clammy and breathless, the sheets drenched with sweat. Saoirse wasn't crying, she didn't need a feed. *I can't do this. I don't know how to be a mother*. Her heart pounded; her stomach turned itself inside out. She checked her again. *I can't do this. I don't know how to be a mother.* Deirdre tried to calm herself, get a few precious hours of sleep, but her mind kept racing. *Something will happen to Saoirse and it will be all my fault. She'll get meningitis or some awful illness and I'll lose her.* As the dawn light started to shine through the bedroom window, she realised she'd spent the whole night checking her, getting up to see if she was still breathing.

You have to pull yourself together, she told herself, it's nothing. You have to distract yourself, you have to get on with it, to think about other things. All new mothers felt like this sometimes. Didn't they?

Chapter Forty-Seven

WEXFORD, 2000

19 November 1998

Dear Sister Sarto,
I got your name earlier today from _____ *of the*
Adoption Board. I am writing to make information available
in the case of my son who was born in your home on the
16th June 1981. My name is Deirdre Wadding and I was
eighteen at the time of his birth. I believe the Sr in charge is
no longer with you but I'm told Sr Justine is there and it's
possible she would remember me.

At the time of staying in the Sacred Heart home, I was
studying for a teaching diploma and studied during the day

in a room in the courtyard between the two residences. I used the name Ciara while waiting for my baby to be born.

I would very much like to meet my son if he should wish to make contact with me. I named him Paul but I understand (in a letter shortly after birth from Sister Justine), he was christened Mark. He will be eighteen next June and I felt this might be a good time for me to put information on record for him to access when (and if) he is ready. I'm aware of the many pressures on teenagers these days and the dangers of drugs and alcohol. I certainly don't want to place any extra pressure or anxieties on Mark or his family but on the other hand perhaps making myself available to him will help him to deal with some of the issues which might bother him at this age.

I am now married. It is, in fact, my second marriage. I have been dealing with the emotional repercussions of giving my son up for very many years and feel that the pressure of secrecy and having a double life took quite a toll over the years. At the time of placing my son for adoption, I truly believed that I had no other option and that he would have a better life without me.

I was heartbroken leaving him and became obsessed with having another baby which I could keep. I actually did become pregnant the following year and had another son in 1982 but I was far from emotionally sorted out at the time and felt I couldn't do it to my parents again so I went to another mother and baby home in County Meath and again placed my second son Diarmuid for adoption. Diarmuid is a half-brother to Mark and is sixteen years old today.

The cumulative emotional effect of the two losses was huge and greatly affected me for many years. I believe that at the time of my first marriage in 1987 I had still not resolved my feelings about letting my children go. I have never for one day stopped thinking about them. I remarried in 1992 and am now very happy and feel that I have come a long way. I've been through blaming my parents for putting pressure on me, blaming myself for not being strong enough or courageous enough to keep my sons and finally coming to terms with the fact that I did what I believed was best at the time and also the fact that I still regret not having my son with me all these years.

I can never have that time back and I don't expect anything from Mark but I hope to have the opportunity to meet him and answer any questions he may have about me or about his father. It would of course be a tremendous bonus if we formed any kind of bond or relationship.

I now within my second marriage have two children, a daughter Saoirse (who is five and knows that when her mammy was younger she had two boys which she was unable to provide for and who were adopted) and a son Tuan, who is eight and a half months. My husband, Graham, is a teacher, we met on a special educational needs diploma course in Drumcondra, Dublin. He knows all about Mark and Diarmuid and we have had many talks about them. He is totally supportive of me making contact with them and would be happy to welcome them to our home if either or both of them seek me out.

I will keep a copy of this letter for reference and have also put my address and phone number on file with the Adoption Board and indicated my receptivity to contact with Mark.

Mark's father's name was P_____, also from Wexford. He was seventeen at the time of the pregnancy and was very vulnerable and I suppose I felt he would be unable to deal with fatherhood. I, at my parents' insistence, never told him of the pregnancy until a year later.

I am no longer in touch but am friendly with his female cousin who knows about Mark. She tells me Mark's father is now married and living in _____ and I imagine it would be easy to get in touch with him if Mark should wish that, in the future.

If possible, I would like my medical records from the Convent Hospital as I may have a gap in my obstetric history, not being clear exactly what happened during Mark's birth. I know I was induced and had a forceps delivery and now appear to have a lot of scar tissue. It would be helpful to know which procedures were followed during labour and birth.

Yours with thanks,
Wishing you love and light,
Deirdre Wadding

❖

11 February 1999

Dear Mrs Wadding,
Thank you for your recent letter.
I have put a note on Mark's file that you will be writing to us after June 16th.
When you are writing to us, please quote the reference Cork 98 Wadding.

With best wishes
Your sincerely,
Sister Sarto

15 June 1999

Dear Deirdre,
Further to your letter today, I contacted Mark's parents to inform them of your request. They told me that Mark is currently in the United States and will be home in September and will begin his first year in college. He sat for his Leaving Certificate last year and took the year off before applying for a place in college. I will contact you in September. If you don't hear from me, feel free to ring or write.

With best wishes, yours sincerely,
Sister Sarto

8 February 2000

Dear Deirdre,
Thank you for your letter of 25th January regarding your son, Mark. I'm sorry you were unable to contact me when you phoned recently. I've checked through the communications that we have had with each other. My last letter to you states that we had put your request on file

and Mark should be notified when he was eighteen years. I contacted the home and spoke to his adopted father, who said he was in America, but when he returned home he would speak to him about your request. I had no further communication with the family until this morning, when I rang the home again. His father answered the phone, he was very pleasant and I read bits of your letter to him. He told me that he did convey the message to Mark when he came home, but he appeared not to be interested at that time. I asked if he had returned to the States again. 'No,' he said, 'he is here in bed, sound asleep.' He said he would speak to Mark again today and see what he says. I asked if Mark would come and see me, so that I could have some idea of his feelings. 'He is very much his own man,' he said, and, 'Yes, that would be a good idea.' I promise to let you know what response, if any, I get from this conversation. Wishing you every blessing for 2000.

With best wishes, yours sincerely,
Sister Sarto

Juggling baby Tuan on her hip, Deirdre looked through all of the correspondence again, a pile of letters and reference numbers and files. Normally she liked this time of the morning, the calmness after 9 a.m. when Graham had gone to work, her daughter Saoirse was safely deposited at the school gates, and she could have a cup of tea and a few precious minutes of peace before starting into the day's tasks.

Things had been easier this time with Tuan, after a rocky start. The birth had been difficult. His shoulders got stuck, the cord wrapped around his neck, and he had to spend a week in an incubator; it took three days before Deirdre stopped shaking when she went in and out of the hospital. But she didn't have the months of panic and nightmares that she'd had with Saoirse. When she went for medical appointments she looked the doctors squarely in the eye and said he was her fourth child. And she'd learned to go easier on herself, that she didn't have to watch over her children's every waking moment so intently.

Looking at the wad of paper on the kitchen table, she sighed; it didn't matter how many times she went over it, the facts remained the same. She hadn't progressed one iota in her mission to be reunited with her son.

'He appeared not to be interested at that time.' There was no way that could be misinterpreted; there was no way she had got it wrong. She rescued one of the pages from Tuan's chubby hands. At least she had a new photograph. His adoptive parents had sent it via the convent; Paul, or Mark, rather, was now a handsome young man, tall and broad-shouldered with very dark hair, brown eyes and dimples showing on both cheeks as he smiled. He had a strong face, with each feature well defined. She would put it with the others in the album: the baby photos, her wedding photos, the ones of Saoirse on her first day at school. Saoirse already knew about the two brothers who didn't live with her, and Tuan would understand too when he was older; she had no intention of keeping it a secret.

Mark was nearly nineteen, the same age she had been when she'd lost him, on her nineteenth birthday. *I was so innocent then*, she thought, *so young and so utterly broken.* And even all these years later, when she could talk about it openly with her father, her sister and her husband, the images of Bessborough sometimes returned when she least expected it. *A row of cots, a set of stone steps.* Or she got a flash of the staircase, so clean and smelling of bleach; sometimes the most mundane of domestic tasks would trigger it. Or she remembered a snippet of the car journey home when she left Paul/Mark behind in Cork, and she thought a part of her soul had been left behind there too.

Chapter Forty-Eight

WEXFORD, 2000

'Deirdre? Deirdre Wadding?' said a voice. In her local pub, Deirdre turned around to see a man standing beside her; he looked vaguely familiar, perhaps around the eyes, but she couldn't be sure.

'Yes ... hi,' she said, still struggling to place him.

She'd escaped the kids for a few hours and had come in to meet a friend who worked in the health food shop but now she had been drawn into a trip down memory lane. It was embarrassing; she'd find out in a minute who he was and would kick herself.

He smiled. 'You don't remember me. I'm Patrick.'

He looked very different from the young man who'd gone

to Carnsore Point with her all those years ago, the summer before she'd been in Bessborough. Gone was the thick hair and the angular features; his hair had thinned and he had filled out over the years.

'Patrick! I haven't seen you in so long,' she stuttered, trying to steer the conversation back onto the right track. She hadn't laid eyes on him for years; she'd heard he'd got married, had started a family.

'Listen, can I have a quick word?' he asked. 'I never asked you very much about what happened back then. When you told me, I just accepted it. I wasn't very curious.'

'Come on,' she said, picking up the glasses of wine from the counter. 'My friend knows all about it, so we can speak freely.'

'I've a lot to tell you,' she said when they'd settled into a quiet corner. 'I've started looking for him.'

She filled him in on the letters and phone calls, the photographs she had been sent of him as a baby, what she knew of the family and that, by all accounts, he'd been living a happy life.

Patrick was quiet. 'I know it's a lot to take in,' she told him.

'I think you should be able to meet him and if I can help you, I will,' he said slowly, reaching for his pint.

Deirdre hesitated. 'This is a small town. You're married, you have kids – does your wife know all about this? I don't want to cause any problems.'

'She knows. I told her everything from the beginning. You don't need to worry about that.'

He reached in his pocket, pulling out his business card with his address and home phone number on it. 'Will you send me copies of everything? I'm going to write to the convent and say I want to send a letter to him, with confirmation that they have been sent on to his address.'

A few months later, Patrick phoned her.

'Deirdre, I've got some news.' His tone was urgent. 'I've heard from him. I left an email address on the bottom of my letter and he responded.'

'Seriously?'

'He put in a note about you in his email. He said: "Are you in touch with Deirdre? If you are, please apologise that I haven't answered her letters, I'm not much of a letter writer, but if she has an email address, I could get in touch with her."'

Deirdre ended the call and rushed to a friend's house. She didn't have the internet so her friend's husband helped her set up an email address on their dial-up connection. It was her first ever email, and she struggled with it, with the clunky keys, the small pop-up box on a screen, the pressure of finding the right words.

I would love to have a relationship with you, but I want you to be really honest and open with me. If you've ever felt anger or resentment or feelings of abandonment or anything at all, I want you to tell me, because it's been so long that if we're going to have a relationship now, I would want it to be completely honest and open.

A couple of days later, she received her first email back.

No, I don't have any of that, I've always known I was adopted. I've had a really happy life, a really good home, and I think it must've been much harder for you carrying that around all these years. Don't be worrying about emails if it's not your thing.

She read on – he'd left his mobile number at the bottom and her heart soared with relief.

Chapter Forty-Nine

CORK, 2000

Deirdre had a nervous feeling in her stomach all morning. Had it been a good idea? It was so soon. But Mark's emails had been so friendly and relaxed; he hadn't been angry or upset. She was in Cork anyway to visit her aunt, who was in hospital there, and she'd gone with her gut and invited him to go for lunch with her. If he'd said no, she would have understood, but he had accepted immediately, sounded pleased to hear from her. Now she was second-guessing herself. She'd heard that other meetings like this were mediated by a social worker. Would that have been better? she wondered.

She pulled her coat around her; it was December and the wind carried with it a biting chill. He'd suggested the doorway of Brown Thomas, a department store with a limestone facade in the centre of Cork City. The windows had been decorated for Christmas with lots of red ribbon, shiny baubles and tinsel. She had been watching the passers-by for the past five minutes or so, scrutinising every tall man with dark hair for any traces of her son. Then she saw him walking towards her and she knew him immediately. He was tall, confident and broad-shouldered; he broke into a huge smile that dominated his face.

'Hi, Deirdre,' he said.

My God, she thought, this young man is my baby. They hugged. 'It's wonderful, wonderful to finally meet you,' she said, her eyes filling with hot tears. They walked to a local sandwich place, but Deirdre could barely touch what she'd ordered. She felt a rush of excitement running through her veins, and she couldn't stop looking at Mark. It felt natural, like two people who'd known each other for years.

'This is really emotional for me ... but I'm very intense, I verbalise everything,' she said.

Mark smiled. 'I'm really sorry it took me so long to get back to you,' he began. 'I think I might have said to you before, I'm not much of a letter writer. I was in the States, I took a gap year after my Leaving and I needed a bit of time ... I had a great childhood, my parents are amazing. I have a younger sister as well – they adopted a little girl after me.'

Deirdre felt herself relax.

Over lunch she learned about his interests: he loved science and technology and was going to study engineering in UCC. He had a girlfriend, a big group of friends and he seemed settled, comfortable in his own skin. The conversation flowed easily, and she didn't have to try and fill awkward pauses. He didn't ask about Bessborough or make any reference to the long letter she'd written him explaining everything, also telling him about Diarmuid. She suspected that he hadn't accessed his file but she didn't want to get into all of that now. She was enjoying his easy company, wanted to hear everything she could about his life. The food was being cleared away, but she willed him not to notice; she didn't want it to end; she wanted to keep listening to him talk.

'Listen, my local is just around the corner – do you want to go for a drink?' he said.

'I'd love that.' Deirdre was touched that he'd suggested his local, the sort of place that he might bump into someone he knew, and he'd have to introduce her. He wasn't embarrassed by her, she realised, or by having to explain things.

The pub was a mix of a traditional old man's pub with more modern touches. They sat opposite each other at a table near the window, the light streaming in. Deirdre took a sip of her glass of wine, grateful for it. It was so odd in its own way, having a drink in a pub with the baby she'd given up all those years ago.

'I'd really like to meet my other siblings,' he told her. 'That's one of the main reasons I wanted to meet you.'

'Well, you've got Saoirse and Tuan,' she told him. 'Saoirse is seven and Tuan is only two. I'm sure they'd love to get to know you too.' She pictured them in her mind getting so excited to meet an older half-brother, Tuan climbing on top of him, Saoirse begging him to join in one of her games.

As Mark walked with Deirdre back to the bus station, he made a gesture with his hands that immediately reminded her of Patrick, Mark's father; watching him, she was taken back to the summer in Wexford when she was a young college girl, just a year younger than him. The flash disappeared as quickly as it appeared, and she couldn't have picked out the exact characteristic, but she hoped she'd see it again or catch a glimpse of another family member, spot traces of others mapped out in his facial features.

'See you soon,' he told her.

They didn't make any concrete plans and she didn't want to force it. For the moment, she could picture him fully, her first son; she had got an insight into the person he was. That was enough for now, she thought, as she watched his long arms wave her off until he was no longer in sight.

Chapter Fifty

WEXFORD, 2008–11

Dear Daniel*,

It took quite a while to come down to earth after I heard from you ... If you're just taking your time digesting the fact that we're now in touch with each other, then that's absolutely fine and you take as long as it takes. But please, if there's anything at all you need to say to me, then do, even if you think it might be hurtful. I would like us to get to know each other as the real people we are. I'm often told I'm full-on, so I am aware of that aspect of myself and will be fully respectful of your need to let this contact develop at your pace.

I think of you often and always with love. I hope you can fully believe that it was out of love for you and not for the lack of it that I gave you up. Hearing from you was absolutely wonderful. It's a gift and blessing but it also brings with it, as no doubt for you, a mix of emotions. Especially the 'what if' which I have played out in my head many times over the years. It means everything to me that you can say you believe I made the right choice and that you have had a happy life. It's perfect recompense for the loss of you. I can never believe that it was the right thing for me but the fact that you have been happy means that it was a good decision. Of course there are many things I would love to know about you, most of all just who you are as a person and that's not something you can tell me in one email. It's something I will learn gradually. I suppose I'd like to know what are the things that really matter to you. What makes you shine? What do you believe in? What sustains you when you feel low? What do you love to do with your time? ...

I look forward to hearing from you, whenever you feel ready.

With love,
Deirdre

That's it, Deirdre thought. That seems about right. It had taken her at least an hour to compose a response she was happy with, and reading back over it, the tone felt appropriate, not too much. She didn't want to overwhelm him.

Her son Diarmuid, now going by the name Daniel, was twenty-five. The tracing process had started later than with Mark because the Rotunda Girls Aid Society, who arranged Daniel's adoption, had a policy of not facilitating requests until the adopted person was at least twenty-three. A few weeks before, Daniel had been given Deirdre's contact information and had sent her a brief message. And Deirdre had read it again and again, all about his life in the suburbs of a small Australian town; he was a graphic designer by day and a rock musician in the evenings.

Daniel's tone was a little guarded, she thought, but friendly and curious. He had always known that he was adopted, he told her. 'I am forever in your debt for bringing me into this world,' he said. Her choice to allow someone else to raise him, he told her, was brave and difficult for her. Although they could never know how things would have been had her decision been different, Daniel believed that she did the right thing. The last line made her heart give a little leap of joy. 'I am more than happy to exchange emails with you,' he said.

She hit the 'Send' button.

Over the next few months, Daniel sent photos of himself and his wife on their wedding day; he was tall, fair-haired and lean. Deirdre sent photos of herself, now forty-six, of his half-siblings, Saoirse and Tuan, and little Rowan who had been born in 2001, even an old photo of her and Daniel's father, Jack, from back in the day. She told him that her marriage of fifteen years had ended in 2003 and she was adjusting to co-parenting three children, to a new house, with a new job in a health food shop to tide her over.

They wrote every few weeks, pen pals from across the ocean, sending good wishes and snippets of news. Daniel didn't always respond, but when he did, he said that he didn't want to discourage her from contacting him. 'This is all just going to take a bit of time but I'm sure it will get easier for both of us,' he told her in one of his emails.

Deirdre tried not to compare it with her relationship with Mark, with the Mother's Day cards from him that warmed her heart, his attendance at Rowan's blessing ceremony and her trips to Cork. Daniel is a different personality, she told herself, living on the other side of the world. The level of contact is his choice, and I respect that. Every email was a step closer to getting to know him, the start, she hoped, of a long conversation with her second son.

On his twenty-sixth birthday, she sent a message:

Happy birthday, it's so amazing to be able to say that directly to you for the first time in twenty-six years. It's hard to believe twenty-six years have passed.

He thanked her, sent her a photo of him grinning with his new guitar. She sent him more news of his half-siblings.

❖

On Daniel's twenty-ninth birthday, in 2011, Deirdre sat down to write him a message.

Thinking of you today, naturally, hope you had a wonderful day, wishing you love and blessings. Would love to hear how things are with you. Saoirse at college, now does drama. Tuan has started secondary. Rowan in Fourth Class at primary.

She looked through her inbox for the last message she'd received from him. There hadn't been a response for over two years. Enough, she thought. I have to stop.

She read all the messages again, tried in her mind to pinpoint the moment, the exact instant where it started to go wrong, if she'd said or done anything to offend him. There was nothing, at least nothing that was obvious to her. One of his last emails to her said, 'Keep in touch.' He just doesn't want a relationship at the moment, she told herself. I have to accept that.

Chapter Fifty-One

WEXFORD, 2011

'Why are you here today, Deirdre?' Mairead asked.

In the counsellor's small offices in rural Wexford, Deirdre took a deep breath.

'I got into a relationship recently. It was with a man who I was very passionate about, and it was the first time I'd been serious about somebody else since I got divorced from my husband a few years ago.'

'OK. Let's start with the most recent relationship. What went wrong?'

'At the start, it was all going well. He was showering me with affection, he told me I was wonderful, and I was swept away by him. I thought maybe I'd met my soulmate ... But then it all started to go wrong and I had to end it. It's hit me really badly, much harder than I thought.'

'And how has it affected you?'

'I've barely been able to get out of bed, and when I do, I'm crying all the time and not able to deal with anything. And to be honest, it's really confused me. I'm forty-eight; I have a teenage daughter and two younger sons. My middle one, Tuan, has autism and we try hard to support him with the extra challenges that it means for him. And I've gone through lots of other stuff in my life. I don't understand why I've reacted like this.'

'Tell me a bit more about what happened.'

'Well, after a while, he, this man, started to change. He was very angry about things that had happened to him in his life. He talked about some of the other relationships I had had, and he seemed almost too interested in the other men I'd been with; there were little digs here and there. At the start I thought nothing of it, but after a while I started to think he was a bit judgemental, trying to make me feel ashamed about things, putting me down when he got the opportunity. My friends noticed, and they told me that I wasn't quite the same as I used to be.'

'Did you talk to him about his behaviour?'

'Yeah, I did. And he'd explain that he was in therapy, that he'd had a difficult time. And I'd let it go. But after a while, it didn't matter what I did – I was always in the wrong in his eyes. He'd accuse me of flirting with other men so I stopped going out as much to avoid the hassle.'

'Did things get worse, Deirdre?'

'They started to, yes ... he would have these mad outbursts, and they were verbally aggressive, but there was never anything physical. But one evening he screamed at me, he used the c-word, and I hate that word, I think it's disgusting, and he threatened to smash my phone. And he drew himself up and said, "You don't know what I'm capable of." And something in me just thought, "It's over, this is it, we're done." It was like I was drowning in this dark, angry energy that wasn't mine.'

'How did you feel when you broke up?'

'Absolutely depleted – it was like I had been completely emptied out.'

Mairead paused for a second. 'If he was to come back to you now and ask you to get back together, what would you say?'

Deirdre exhaled deeply. 'I'm kind of ashamed to say this to you, but I would say yes because I still really love him, and I really miss him.'

Mairead nodded. 'OK. I want you to think about your daughter. Imagine she had broken up from a relationship where the guy was treating her the same way he was treating you, and behaving in the same way that this man was behaving with you. If she told you she wanted to go back to him, what would you advise her?'

'Oh, God, no. I couldn't have her go back to somebody like that.'

Mairead smiled. 'Before you come back next week, Deirdre, I want you to think about something. Why is this situation OK for you but not for your daughter?'

'I want you to tell me about your first experience in a mother and baby institution, your time in Bessborough,' Mairead asked her in their next session.

Deirdre steadied herself. She had told other people about this before, and her sister and her ex-husband had heard the full unadulterated version over the years, but it was never easy, even with Mairead. She poured it all out: she told her about the house name she went by, the secret letters, the system that would rival the secret service, leaving Paul/Mark behind and how she still felt a mixture of grief and guilt, all these years later.

'In a way, it could be that all these things happened to Ciara and not to Deirdre,' Mairead began.

'How do you mean?'

'When you went into Bessborough as a young girl, you learned to answer to that other name, Ciara, and when you left, you left that identity behind you, to help you cover up the secret. It was almost as if those experiences happened to someone else.'

Deirdre nodded.

'Maybe on some level, it allows you to hive off those experiences and compartmentalise them.'

'I see.'

'Compartmentalising things can be useful, even necessary. You can get back on your feet, you can go back to work, you can continue on with your life. You can continue on quite normally and appear to cope well ... The problem with that though, Deirdre, is that sometimes it all becomes too much and things can start bubbling up and impacting your life ... And sometimes what happens is that you end up not really dealing with things.'

Tears streamed down Deirdre's face.

'I never wanted to give them up but I went along with it ... I wasn't strong enough to stand up to my family, to the nuns, to the social workers, everyone ... I'll always regret that.'

'You've done very well today, Deirdre. But the most important thing to remember is that it's not your fault, what happened to you when you were eighteen. You have to stop blaming yourself.'

❖

'It's been a tough nine months for you, Deirdre. You've worked really hard.'

Deirdre had come to the end of her time with Mairead, and though she still had bad days, she was in a much better place.

'Those feelings had been buried for a long time. Thank you for everything, Mairead. You've helped me so much.'

As she made her way to the car, Deirdre thought about all of the exercises Mairead had taken her through: in one, Deirdre verbalised all of the things she never got a chance to say to her mother when she was alive. As the sessions progressed, she learned to forgive her, to see her as a product of her time and her upbringing, to remember the good times she had with her.

They'd also devoted hours to the residual shame that Deirdre felt about losing two children to adoption, how it affected her self-esteem. Just because she had been open with people close to her in her life, it didn't mean that she had dealt with feelings of unworthiness. Part of the work was realising that she was entitled to consider that she had been badly treated by the system; for years, she had graded her experience against the experiences of women of previous generations. 'I didn't work in a laundry, and I found out where my children were. So many other women didn't,' she'd told Mairead. 'What I went through is nothing compared to what other women had to put up with.'

'But you lost your children too, Deirdre. The outcome was the same,' the counsellor had said. And Deirdre had started to see that she too suffered loss, banishment, judgement, shame, trauma and grief; a softer version, perhaps, in a slightly more modern Ireland.

In another session she'd talked about reuniting with Mark, how he had recently moved to the US for work and the contact between them had become less frequent. She was so grateful to his parents for making him the person that he was, kind and thoughtful and generous. But she still felt conflicted. 'I wasn't the mother who reared him, who cared for him when he was sick, who took him to his sports events. I'll never be that person,' she told Mairead. With Daniel, she felt rejected; Mairead taught her to experience those feelings as they occurred, not to push them away or pretend that everything was OK.

One of the last things they'd dealt with was how her past experiences had affected her marriage to Graham. The period of searching for her sons had put pressure on their relationship. 'I just withdrew, you know? I don't know if my marriage would have broken down if I had understood my feelings back then. I just felt so empty,' she told Mairead. It had caused tensions, corroded the close bond they'd built up over the years. And Mairead had helped her see that the tracing process had brought her back to her time in mother and baby institutions, and she'd repeated the behaviour she developed then of compartmentalising, of retreating into herself, of shutting others out and trying to pretend everything was OK.

But there was one part of her own story that even chatting with Mairead couldn't help with. It was a secret she wasn't quite sure was a secret, and if it was, she didn't know if it was hers to tell. When she moved back to Wexford when her children were born, Jack, the father of Daniel, was living there with his wife and their children. Her children were friends with Jack's children; they were in school together, shared some of the same classes, hung around together like classmates do. Jack and his wife had since split up, but Deirdre knew his ex-wife, a woman she liked and respected. She was never sure if the other family knew they had a half-brother in common.

I'm still not being entirely truthful about my own situation, she thought as she drove back to the cottage. It really got to her, having to keep things from her own children.

Chapter Fifty-Two

WEXFORD, 2021

An unknown number popped up on Deirdre's phone in the middle of the January lockdown. She hesitated for a second. It's probably about the opinion piece I wrote in the *Wexford People* about the mother and baby institutions, she thought. Deirdre had been pleased with it – she felt she had got her points across well and it had been picked up by the *Irish Independent*. But she hadn't included any information about the second adoption or her experience of Dunboyne.

'For a number of reasons of ethical complexity I only share the details of the first experience in Bessborough, something I hope to change this year,' she had written. She had agonised over that line.

She picked up the phone.

'Hello,' she said, a tad tentatively.

'Deirdre, it's Jack.'

'Jack, hi—' She hadn't heard from him in years, not since his marriage had broken up. The last she'd heard, he hadn't been in contact with his family for a long time.

'Listen, I saw your article in the paper,' he began. 'I want to apologise to you. I should have done it ages ago. And I should have been there for you all those years ago.'

'Thank you,' she said. Even after all this time, it was still meaningful to hear a sincere apology. She took a deep breath. 'Listen, Jack, have you ever told your family? Our kids are really good friends.'

'No. They don't know my story.'

'It's not just your story. They have a right to know.'

'They don't need to know.'

Deirdre put down the phone, defeated. It's a life sentence, all this, she thought. There's always something. I'll never be fully free of it.

She sat with it for a few days, feeling shaky about the whole thing. Now she knew for certain that the other family had never been told about Daniel, and that Jack had no intention of ever telling them.

❖

A few days later, Jack's ex-wife phoned. Her voice was tense and Deirdre braced herself.

'Deirdre, I'm just ringing to say that keeping all this a secret should not have been on you,' she told her.

Deirdre felt herself relax. 'That's really generous of you,' she said slowly. 'Thank you for being so good about it.'

'I'm just annoyed with him really. He should have told us. And you should not have had to carry that.'

'Do the kids know?'

'They took it really well. Nobody has any bad feelings towards you. They're just glad to know and they're taking it in. For the moment, they don't want to pursue it any further or go down the route of talking to social workers.'

'I'm so glad to hear that. I'm just happy that they have a choice.'

Later that evening, Deirdre posted the images she had of Mark and Daniel as babies on her Facebook page, explaining how she had lost them as a teenage girl. 'Every family has their photos on the shelf ... ours has two who didn't grow up with this family but are always remembered ...' she wrote. The comments came flooding in. 'We hold them in our hearts,' wrote a friend. 'Beautiful children,' wrote another. 'You speak so deeply for so many ... your heart was broken,' said someone else. Comment after comment expressed good wishes and solidarity, and finally Deirdre felt she could speak openly about both experiences, with

no chance that it would affect another family. She cried
as she read the messages. It was unlikely that her children
would ever be in a room with one another, she thought.
She'd never have a photograph of all of them together –
every wedding, every graduation, every celebration will go
ahead without Daniel.

Chapter Fifty-Three

WEXFORD, 2021

Deirdre woke up on her fifty-ninth birthday, 19 June, and looked out the window of her cottage in south Wexford; the early-morning sun was rising over the lush southern countryside, the pink light mixing with the grey clouds and turning to a confident yellow. She took her time observing the view; her schedule was free of the online workshops she gave as a trainer in her own school of spirituality. She got dressed, slipping away without waking Ronan*, her partner of nine years whom she'd met after she'd done all that work with Mairead. I'll just take a few moments, she thought, a walk to clear my head before the day starts in earnest.

Outside, the air was still crisp and she gathered her cardigan around herself as she got into the car. Parking by the harbour of her local beach, she opted for her favourite cliff walk high among the dunes, by the patches of blazing yellow gorse. She stopped for a moment, looking out over the sea, the waves crashing into the shore. In the distance she could see the Tuskar Rock Lighthouse, its white granite tower firmly rooted to the rock beneath.

The walk was calm, quiet; apart from the occasional dog-walker, she almost had it to herself. It was always the same at this time of year; she couldn't help thinking about her time in Bessborough; Mark's birthday had been three days ago. Four decades had gone by and she still saw her life in two parts: before Bessborough and after Bessborough. It wasn't normal, she thought, to have days where you can't really move, get out of bed, talk to anyone. Nor for a scene from a run-of-the-mill TV drama to bring back those images of the day she left Paul/Mark behind in Bessborough. *A row of cots, a set of stone steps, the sound of a car door closing.* I haven't fully dealt with everything, she thought. I need more help. And as she walked down from the dunes and back to the car, she made a promise to herself that she'd go back to counselling.

Back at the cottage, the rest of the day passed as peacefully as it could in a house with five adults, two cats and four kittens. Later in the evening, Mark called from the US.

'Happy birthday,' he said. She could hear Mark's wife and their little son Billy's* voice chiming in on the good wishes.

'You're making me feel old now, what with you turning forty this year,' she told him, and he laughed. They talked about his work and Covid and the housing crisis, a deep chat you can only have with someone close.

'Put me on to the others,' he said. 'I want to say hello to them too.' And as she watched Saoirse, Tuan and Rowan, students living back home with Deirdre for lockdown, have a relaxed chat with their half-brother, it struck her that Mark had been in her life longer than he had been missing from it. Our relationship is so strong now, she thought. I'm not the mammy or the granny to Billy but I have a role in their lives, we're so connected.

In the evening, Saoirse made a bean and potato casserole and a salad, and the family sat outside, passing around the plates, drinking prosecco with the sun setting under the Wexford sky, watching the changing colours of the late-evening clouds.

'Let's take a photo,' Deirdre said, gathering them around her, draping her arms around their shoulders, grinning as they crouched in for a selfie. As day turned to night and she caught a glimpse of the moon, she was reminded for a second of the missing son, Daniel. Maybe he's just waking up in Australia, she thought. She wished him light, love and happiness.

Epilogue

London, February 2022

Joan, Terri and Deirdre. Three women whose experiences of Bessborough as teenage girls left them utterly changed. Though they had very different personalities, generational perspectives and backgrounds, they had in common an openness that was rare. As the manuscript progressed, I shared draft chapters with each of them, and they offered their own feedback. Deirdre, with her love of language, suggested word substitutions to make passages more authentic.

All three admitted that they found it strange, reading about their own lives on the page, but they did not skip over the most difficult sections. Joan liked being drawn into the story and wanted to emphasise the tenacity she had shown in overcoming so many obstacles to find Walter. 'That's my bold personality, really, as well as my defiance,' she told me. She also wanted to be honest about the challenges that she had faced in reconnecting with her adult son. 'A lot of mothers are reluctant to say how it is ... they think that they might have failed ...' she explained. She talked about how in later years the shame of what had happened to her was lifted when she spoke publicly about her experiences or campaigned on the issue. 'It was as if you opened my diaphragm up and took away years of pain. It was marvellous. It was liberating.'

Terri's interviews were filled with a longing and a hope, however remote, that she would one day meet her son Niall. She wanted to highlight the psychological impact of losing a child to adoption at a time when mental health or mother and baby institutions weren't openly talked about in Ireland. 'I tried my best to be the person that I should be, you know, the wife, the mother, the sister, the daughter. But it wasn't Terri. I lost Terri in Bessborough,' she explained. And when she looked back, she saw that it was only in her forties that she recognised that the nightmares, the images of Niall that popped into her head, were part of a lasting trauma. 'I had loads of triggers ... But I didn't recognise flags, because I didn't know that there was a way of avoiding triggers ... So all of that came much later for me.' And through her studies in the social sciences, she slowly began to realise that 'the shame belongs to the people who allowed this to happen'.

Deirdre told me she sometimes ended up in tears when

she read her sections. Most of all, she had wanted to stress the impact her experiences of mother and baby institutions had had on her future relationships. 'The reality ... is deep, deep trauma, deep grief, deep loss, devastation, and an imprint that led to huge issues within relationships, two broken marriages ... That passes on into your parenting ... There was a lot of deep-rooted stuff, I think, in me, that was fearful that I would get it wrong,' she said. 'The shame for me as I grew older was that I wasn't strong enough, that I didn't just find a way [to keep my children]. Then I have to catch myself and go, "I wasn't who I am now, then."'

Despite their openness, I knew that it had not been easy for Joan, Terri and Deirdre to speak with me, and I had a huge admiration for their decision to give evidence to the Commission of Investigation into Mother and Baby Homes – an inquiry set up in 2015 to examine the treatment of unmarried mothers and their children between 1922 and 1998. The commission had been extended a number of times and Joan, Terri and Deirdre were very frustrated by this; it emerged as a frequent theme in our conversations. Most of the 550 people who contributed spoke to – or, in Deirdre's case, wrote a letter to – a Confidential Committee. A smaller number of individuals, including Joan and Terri, appeared before an Investigative Committee and had to swear an oath before a judge. This meant that they were robustly questioned and their evidence was challenged. From the outset, campaigners had criticised the way the commission operated. Dr Maeve O'Rourke and Claire McGettrick of the Clann Project had repeatedly pointed out that its terms of reference were very narrow, excluding institutions such as private nursing homes and maternity hospitals involved in adoptions, and that the inquiry did not take a human-rights-centred approach to analysing the evidence it was gathering.[25]

On 12 January 2021, the commission issued its final report. It ran to almost 3,000 pages, a litany of misogyny and oppression in terse, sometimes ambiguous language. It detailed the cold atmosphere of large institutions, the harsh treatment, and sometimes emotional abuse, of Irish women and girls, who endured longer stays in mother and baby institutions than their European counterparts. It acknowledged the 'discrimination' faced by children born in the institutions as a result of being born outside marriage; it pointed out that girls under the age of consent were frequently admitted and that there was no evidence to suggest the men who raped them were routinely reported to the gardaí. The commission said it had received 'very few records' from the congregation of the Sisters of the Sacred Hearts of Jesus and Mary, who ran Bessborough.

A total of 923 children and 31 women died in Bessborough in the years it was in operation. As was widely expected, the commission had not uncovered any more information about where they were buried since the fifth interim report was published almost two years before. No burial records can be found for 19 of the missing women and 859 of the children even though canon law required records to be retained. The commission said it was 'highly likely that burials did take place on the grounds' and 'found it very hard to believe' that no one in the congregation of the Sisters of the Sacred Hearts of Jesus and Mary knew where 859 children and 19 women whose burial places were unaccounted for were buried.[26] Sister Mary McManus, who worked in Bessborough between 1948 until it closed in 1999, told the commission that she had no recollection of any deaths during her time there, despite her name being recorded as an informant on the death certificates of a number of children.

The commission's findings were hugely controversial. It said that there was 'no evidence' that women were forced to enter the institutions, 'no evidence' that women were denied pain relief during birth and that the work they did in institutions 'was generally work they had to do if they were living at home'. It did not find evidence that the religious orders made any financial gain from the mother and baby institutions and concluded that there was 'no evidence' that adoptions were forced, while also acknowledging that women and girls would have had no other choice. 'Some of this cohort of women are of the opinion that their consent was not full, free and informed. However, with the exception of a small number of legal cases, there is no evidence that this was their view at the time of the adoption ... The Commission is satisfied that, at least from the 1970s and 1980s, there were adequate procedures in place for ensuring that a mother's consent was full, free and informed,' it concluded.

Another section of the report blamed society, rather than church and state, for the way unmarried mothers in Ireland and their children were treated. 'Responsibility for that harsh treatment rests mainly with the fathers of their children and their own immediate families. It was supported by, contributed to, and condoned by the institutions of the State and the Churches. However, it must be acknowledged that the institutions under investigation provided a refuge – a harsh refuge in some cases – when the families provided no refuge at all,' it stated. Women confined to the institutions were also 'free to leave' at any time.

The commission said there was 'no evidence' of discrimination in the treatment of mixed-race children, Traveller children or children with disabilities,[27] and 'no evidence' that vaccine trials, many of which were carried out in the Bessborough home, caused 'injury' to those who were subjected to them as children, though it acknowledged that 'consent was not obtained from either the mothers of the children or their guardians and the necessary licences were not in place'. Neither could the commission prove or disprove whether 'large sums of money were given to the institutions and agencies in Ireland that arranged foreign adoptions'. In a further controversial statement, the testimonies given by some survivors to the Confidential Committee were described by the commission as 'clearly incorrect ... This contamination probably occurred because of meetings with other residents and inaccurate media coverage'.

The following day, the government gave a public apology. Taoiseach Micheál Martin called the report 'the definitive account of how this country responded to the particular needs of single women and their children at a time when they most needed support and protection'. He said that the time had come for Irish society 'to recognise a profound failure of empathy, understanding and basic humanity over a very lengthy period ... The lack of respect for your fundamental dignity and rights as mothers and children who spent time in these institutions is humbly acknowledged and deeply regretted... The State failed you, the mothers and children in these homes'.

The Sisters of the Sacred Hearts of Jesus and Mary issued their own apology. 'We want to sincerely apologise to those who did not get the care and support they needed and deserved. It is a matter of great sorrow to us that babies died while under our care ... We are distressed and saddened that it is so difficult to prove with legal certainty where many of these infants were buried especially with regard to Bessborough. We did everything possible including the engagement of a professional historian to assist us in our dealings with the

Commission on this vitally important matter ... We also wish to recognise and place on record that many of our Sisters over the decades dedicated their lives and worked tirelessly in providing care for women and children, with limited State support in the early decades,' they said in a statement. As the weeks and months rolled on, apologies were issued from local authorities and the Irish Association for Social Workers. Some survivors accessed the transcripts of their evidence given to the commission and said their testimony was incorrectly recorded. The constant news coverage of the controversy made Joan and Terri weary, and Deirdre posted on Facebook that she needed to take some time out.

After they had time to let things sink in, I arranged to speak to all three women separately about how they felt about the report. On Skype from Cork, Joan said she felt a tension around her temples when she thought about the report's findings. 'The inside of my head was just so tight,' she explained. 'I thought, is this real?'

She told me how she found the process of giving evidence to the Investigative Committee very difficult. 'I remember them saying to me, "Joan, you signed records." I said, "I didn't" ... I got very upset ... I came out of the Baggot Street office and I thought, "I wonder, did they believe everything?"' Since then, she has been working her way through the report but has had to take long breaks. 'People put themselves through opening up old wounds ... for the right reasons – to expose the collusion between church and state and everybody else who was involved ... There is a grave injustice here and I can't let it go,' she told me.

From Dublin, Terri's voice sounded defeated. 'They should have just put their hands up and said the whole lot happened and not defend it ... nobody wants to admit the cruelty involved.' Having told the commission about her experience of being repatriated from the UK, she didn't accept the finding that there was no evidence that women were forced to enter the homes. 'I use words like kidnapping, abduction and maltreatment ... nobody had the right to take me out of one jurisdiction and put me back into another.'

On the phone from Wexford, Deirdre called it a 'whitewash'. 'It is literally outrageous when there are women who will tell you that their children were taken out of their arms ... What was the point in us all pouring our hearts out, sharing our personal grief and details? What an absolute slap in the face.' She took issue with the finding that society was to blame, rather than state and church. 'The people in it are conditioned by the way things are organised around them ... the church and state decided that this is how society is going to work.' She didn't feel that the apologies made any difference to her. 'It doesn't alter anything. Does it give me my child back? Does it give me that time back? Does it take away that pain, grief, loss? No.'

In the months following the report, An Garda Síochána said it did not contain enough detail on its own to warrant a criminal investigation. The garda commissioner encouraged people affected to come forward to a dedicated team, while also warning that the actions taken could be limited, as so much time has passed and witnesses have died. A group of survivors initiated High Court challenges in an attempt to quash some of the findings of the commission's report. They claimed their evidence had been misrepresented and argued that, as they were readily identifiable from the report, they should have been given a right of reply before it was published.[28] The group included Philomena Lee, now eighty-eight – whose experience in the Sean Ross Abbey mother and baby institution was made into an Oscar-nominated movie, *Philomena*, starring Judi Dench – and Mary Harney, born in Bessborough in 1949. Ms Lee's and Ms Harney's cases were chosen as test cases that would set a precedent for the other cases.

In the meantime, most of the archive of the Commission of Investigation has been sealed for thirty years, though survivors and adopted people can request the information the state holds on them from the archive under GDPR (data protection) legislation. But some have said that parts of their own personal information is being withheld until their GP is consulted as to whether it should be released to them.

The *Irish Examiner* reported that people who were part of vaccine trials as children are not being proactively informed that they were involved. Many people remain unaware that they were part of trials.[29] The religious orders retain their own archives.

Despite the controversy, the authors of the commissioner's report refused invitations to appear before a parliamentary committee to answer questions about the findings and cannot be compelled to do so under Irish law. In June 2021, one of the report's authors, Professor Mary Daly, accepted an invitation from Oxford University to take part in an online discussion about the commission. In it, she revealed that the 550 testimonies collected by the Confidential Committee were not used to inform the findings of the report, as they were not given under oath.[30] 'Anything in the main report of the Commission had to meet robust legal standards of evidence,' she explained. Professor Daly also spoke of the 'looming' threat of legal action which led the commissioners to be 'ultra-careful' with what they published. 'If we wrote something that was averse or critical about an individual or an entity, an institution, we had to write a draft report, send them that draft report where we made these critical observations and supply them with the accompanying documentation. And they had a chance to read that, and they had a chance to come back,' she told those in attendance.

The comments led to calls from survivors' groups, Amnesty

International and members of the opposition to repudiate the findings of the commission. These have been rejected by the government, though Minister for Children, Equality, Disability, Integration and Youth Roderic O'Gorman sent a personal email to survivors telling them that he believed them.

Over the next few months, we had further conversations as the mother and baby institutions continued to dominate the news agenda.

In November 2021, the government announced the details of a redress scheme which is expected to open for applications in late 2022. About 34,000 people will be eligible for the ex-gratia payment scheme, which does not require the admittance of liability. Proposed payments will begin at €5,000 up to a maximum payment of €125,000, which is likely to apply only to very few people. All mothers who spent time in a mother and baby institution will be eligible, but people born in the institutions will only be entitled to a payment if they spent more than six months there. Mothers who worked in Bessborough will be ineligible for a work payment unless they had been sent outside the institution to do commercial work. Those who spent more than six months in the home will also be entitled to a form of enhanced medical card but people who were boarded out as children and experienced abuse were controversially not included in the payment scheme.

The government has also indicated that it will seek a financial contribution from the religious bodies involved in the homes,[31] though it is unclear how much the contribution will actually be. Anyone who avails of the redress scheme will have to sign a waiver preventing them from taking legal action in the future.

Announcing the scheme, Minster O'Gorman said: 'It represents a significant milestone in the state's acknowledgment of its past failures and of the needless suffering experienced by so many of its citizens.' Joan, Terri and Deirdre disagreed. They felt all children separated from their natural mothers should be entitled to a payment, regardless of the amount of time spent in the institution, a view echoed by thirty experts in childhood trauma in a letter to the Irish media. 'Early separation from a caregiver is intrinsically stressful ... to state that young children, who might have been in mother and baby homes for a period of two to three months early in life, were less impacted than those who spent longer, is simply not scientifically correct,' they wrote. Joan followed all of the media coverage and watched the parliamentary debates from her flat in Cork. 'Honest to God, we have to keep fighting. It's evident the minister says one thing to us and does the opposite, but we have to battle on,' she told me. Deirdre found it 'divisive' for adult adoptees and 'horrendous' that people who had been boarded out as children were not included. Terri felt that her years of campaigning had not been listened to and couldn't see that the commission's report or the redress scheme had led to any real accountability for what happened. 'They got away with it,' she said.

A court settlement brought some solace. A few weeks after the redress scheme was announced, the Irish state admitted in the High Court that the rights of Philomena Lee and Mary Harney (alongside six other survivors) were breached when they were not provided with a draft copy of the commission's report and given a right of reply. As part of the settlement, an acknowledgement by Minister O'Gorman that some survivors do not recognise sections of the report as a 'true and full reflection' of their experiences will be published. It is not yet known whether the cases will have an impact on the redress scheme.

In recent months, Joan had a further battle to access more of her records and find her own version of the truth. Just before Christmas 2020, she applied for her records from the Child and Family Agency to try to find out more about how her son's adoption had proceeded, when she had always insisted that she had never signed any papers. A few months later, the agency sent her a response with her information. The second-last paragraph stated that she had signed a first set of adoption papers in the presence of a nun in Bessborough on 22 January 1968.

No copy of the signed adoption orders was attached and the social worker told Joan she wasn't entitled to one. 'This is where they drive people cuckoo,' she told me, describing her heated exchange on the phone demanding copies of documents which she was told bore her signature. Following the call, she received them two days later by registered post. The first was a bad photocopy of an adoption order signed in Bessborough in the presence of a nun. The second was dated six months later and filled out in the presence of a notary in Portsmouth, where she had gone to stay with her aunt. Joan says she doesn't recognise the signature, in joined-up handwriting, on either paper. 'That's not my writing at all, at all, at all,' she told me. Though she cannot be sure, she suspects that her mother signed the paper on her behalf in Bessborough when she came to visit, and that her aunt signed the second paper in Portsmouth. Getting the final pieces of documentation has brought her a sense of peace. 'I know I didn't sign it,' she told me. 'I'm relieved. All along, what I was saying was the truth.'

On 12 January 2022, exactly one year after the release of the commission's report, a Birth Information and Tracing Bill was published. The bill – which does not use the term 'birth mother' – provides a right of access to birth certificates and early life files for adopted people, people subject to an illegal birth registration and people who were boarded out as children. A tracing service and a statutory contract preference register, for people who wish to make contact or share information, will also be established.

Terri was disappointed in the legislation; she said the terminology used around information access remained 'woolly' and could be open to interpretation. She disagreed with the requirement for adopted people whose natural parents had expressed a no-contact preference to take part in an information session before their personal data could be released to them.[32] She viewed this as discriminatory towards adopted people, who would not have the same unrestricted rights to their information as any other citizen. But Joan was broadly happy with the bill and felt the Minister had delivered where others had failed. Most of all, she wanted 'to see an end to it all, as it's gone on too long now'.

While discussions continue around accountability and access to information, a parallel conversation is emerging about how to remember institutions like Bessborough and the role they played in our recent past. The government has proposed a national memorial and records centre. Conversations around where such a project should be based and managed are at a very early stage and no concrete plans have yet been put in place.

Terri would like a national museum. She imagines a place where living survivors and their relatives, along with members of the public, can go to reflect on the past. On the walls she'd like to see a video installation with interviews of women who had gone through the system. 'It's important,' she says, 'to see the face and hear the voice and look at the eyes. You won't get that in a textbook.' On a local level she'd like a simple memorial in a park in every county. She imagines a grass margin in the shape of a heart, benches placed either side and passers-by sitting down by a small plaque honouring those who have suffered in institutions.

Joan thinks an educational programme that invites survivors to speak in schools, universities and women's groups would be beneficial. 'To hear it first-hand ... it does sink in ... It's now part of our living history and I think it should be told.' Separately, she has prepared a written statement to go on file in the National University of Ireland, Galway as part of the work of the Clann Project. She hopes that one day in the future, maybe in ten, twenty or even a hundred years from now, students and historians will read it and learn from her account. Deirdre, a former teacher, would also like to see the mother and baby institutions being incorporated as part of the national curriculum. She hopes their inclusion would serve 'as a reminder of just how inhumane society can be to the vulnerable ... an illustration of what a society can do to a group of people if they don't fit in with what society has deemed to be the norm'. She would also like to see a full separation of church and state in Ireland, and for religious denominations to no longer be involved in schools, hospitals and public services.

As I write these words, almost a century has passed since

the first women and children entered Bessborough House and its history as a mother and baby institution began. While other institutions sit empty and neglected, or have been razed to the ground to make room for red-brick luxury housing estates, the old mansion is still in use. As of 2020, the house no longer belongs to the Sisters of the Sacred Hearts of Jesus and Mary; after initially putting it up for sale, the congregation gifted it, and an area of about 2.26 hectares, to the Irish state. The property is now used to provide services for vulnerable families as part of the Bessborough Centre; staff have spoken publicly about the difficulties its past legacy poses to doing their work in the present. The board of directors consists of the congregation of the Sisters of the Sacred Hearts of Jesus and Mary.

The future of the wider Bessborough estate is a pressing concern for Joan, Terri and Deirdre. Some has been sold off over the years; as recently as 2020, the congregation sold another section for €6.85 million.[33] In April 2021, mothers and family members of children who died in Bessborough had to appear at a public hearing against a proposal by a developer to build 179 apartments on the grounds of the former estate. Terri testified at the hearing about her fears Bessborough's history would be 'erased'. 'We all have a stake in this ... we lived it. How can generations come to view our real history if there is nowhere for them to go?'

she asked. The proposal was denied planning permission by Ireland's planning authority but survivors' groups have called for a compulsory purchase order to be put on the site to prevent future developments.

Meanwhile, the government has published draft legislation which will provide a lawful basis for the excavation, recovery and analysis of mothers' and babies' remains at sites previously run by religious orders. It will also allow DNA-based identification to be carried out to reunite families with the remains of their relatives.

There are mixed views as to what to do if the question of excavating the grounds of Bessborough arises in the future. For the moment there are no plans to do so. As part of its research, the commission interviewed local witnesses who marked out areas where they believed they had seen graves. But it 'did not consider it feasible to excavate 60 acres not to mention the rest of the former 200-acre estate', as no 'significant surface evidence' of systematic burial was found. Campaign group the Cork Survivors and Supporters Alliance seeks the 'maintenance, preservation and memorialisation' of an area marked as 'Children's Burial Ground' on historic maps of the Bessborough estate, but is opposed to exhumations.[34] Other family members of the dead wish for a full investigation into the deaths and do not rule out excavations or exhumations if evidence of human remains is found in the future. Joan, Terri and Deirdre think any decision is best left up to mothers and family members of those who died.

The last time I visited Bessborough, on a drizzly November day, I stood in front of the old mansion for a moment. The house was greyer in real life than in the photo I kept on my desk, with spots of rust on the old conservatory and deep cracks over the cut-stone windows. I thought of Joan, Terri and Deirdre, of all the stories of courage I'd had the privilege to hear. They had taught me that the country I had grown up in was so much harsher for women, girls and their children than I had ever imagined, a country where people still struggle to find out the truth about what happened to them and their relatives and grapple every day with the impact of a lifelong loss.

Perhaps in another hundred years, the house will still stand, and the stories from behind its walls will have a different theme. For the moment, at least, it is a reminder of the thousands of women like Joan, Terri and Deirdre who had their motherhood cruelly interrupted and their families split apart.

The congregation of the Sisters of the Sacred Hearts of Jesus and Mary sent this statement on 3 June 2021:

We have no information which could verify any of the allegations contained in your correspondence so in the interests of fairness and justice to all involved we must question all of these allegations ... We also advise that you refer to the recent Commission Report, which had our fullest cooperation, where you will find that some of the matters you raise have been examined. You will also be aware that all records from the Mother and Baby Homes were passed to Túsla (Irish Child and Family Agency) in 2011.

Acknowledgements

I owe my sincerest thanks to Joan, Terri and Deirdre for allowing me to hear their innermost thoughts. Their courage and generosity were limitless and it has been a privilege to get to know them. I am incredibly grateful to all of the other survivors, adopted people and their relatives who gave me their time and expertise for my BBC projects including: 'Bridget', 'Caroline', 'Claire', 'Jess', 'Maria', Rosemary Adaser, Noelle Brown, Conrad Bryan, Carmel Cantwell, Catherine Coffey O'Brien, Oona Collin, Ann Crowe, Anne M. Harris, Jude Hughes, Jessica Kavanagh, Mary Linehan-Foley, Matthew Moynihan, Peter Mulryan, Kathleen Mulryan, Marguerite Penrose, Mari Steed and many more.

Thank you also to Dr Sarah-Anne Buckley, Dr Cathleen Callanan, Beth Carthy, Conall Ó Fátharta, Professor Lindsey Earner-Byrne, Dr James Gallen, Dr Paul Michael Garrett, Dr Lorraine Grimes, Susan Lohan from the Adoption Rights Alliance, Donal O'Keefe, Alison O'Reilly,

Dr Maeve O'Rourke, Dr Jennifer Redmond and Professor James Smith for their insights and swift responses to my questions while researching this subject for the BBC. I am also grateful to the expert who spoke to me off the record.

The Clann Project, the Coalition of Mother and Baby Homes Survivors, the Association of Mixed-Race Irish, the Cork Survivors and Supporters Alliance, Aitheantas, the Society of Survivors and Conall Ó Fátharta published their research online, and in different ways, their work proved to be an incredibly useful resource. And though I read many books and articles while completing this project, I must acknowledge the following sources in particular: *Mother and Child: Maternity and Child Welfare in Dublin 1922–1960* by Professor Lindsey Earner-Byrne; *CLANN: Ireland's Unmarried Mothers and their Children: Gathering the Data: Principal Submission to the Commission of Investigation into Mother and Baby Homes* by Maeve O'Rourke, Claire McGettrick, Rod Baker, Raymond Hill et al.; *The Light in the Window* by June Goulding; *Republic of Shame: Stories from Ireland's Institutions for Fallen Women* by Caelainn Hogan and *Banished Babies: The Secret History of Ireland's Baby Export Business* by Mike Milotte.

My wonderful agent Abi Fellows saw the value in this project from the very beginning; every day, she moves mountains for her authors and makes publishing a kinder, more inclusive place. I'm also deeply grateful to BBC editors

Angus Foster, Finlo Nelson-Rohrer and Malcom Balen; to dear friends Miriam Brosnan, Megha Mohan and Saorlaith Ni Bhroin; to the Society of Authors Antonia Fraser Fund and to the Women's Irish Network for helping me out of a tight financial spot.

The team at Hachette Ireland created a space for these important stories to be shared. Editor Ciara Doorley brought out the best in the manuscript with her wise guidance; Susan McKeever and Aonghus Meaney honed the final drafts into something far better than I could ever have come up with. Elaine Egan, Sharon Plunkett and Mark Walsh took great care in ensuring media coverage was sensitive and appropriate.

Finally, I wish to thank my family, Patricia, Tom, Fionnuala and Diarmaid, for fostering in me a love of reading, stories and words. They have always been my greatest cheerleaders and without them I could never have written this book.

Endnotes

All URLs correct at the time of writing.

1   Records Joan later obtained showed she had been tested for syphilis.

2   M.H. MacInerney, 'The Souper Problem in Ireland' (1922), *Irish Ecclesiastical Record*, 55 (1), pp.140–56.

3   Department of Children, Equality, Disability, Integration and Youth, *Final Report of the Commission of Investigation into Mother and Baby Homes* (2021), https://assets.gov.ie/118565/107bab7e-45aa-4124-95fd-1460893dbb43.pdf, pp.1005–39.

4   The names of the children who died in Bessborough were collected by journalist Donal O'Keefe, who kindly shared his work with me.

5   At least 145 children were adopted by families in the US from Bessborough, mostly between the mid-1940s and the late 1960s. Former RTÉ journalist Mike Milotte investigated the practice and found that little effort was made to investigate American adoptive parents' suitability to rear children. See Mike Milotte, *Banished Babies: The secret story of Ireland's baby export business* (New Island, 1997), pp.12–31.

6 Dr Valerie O'Brien & Dr Sahana Mitra, *An Overview of Adoption Policy and Legislative Change in Ireland 1952–2017* (Adoption Authority of Ireland, 2018), p.7. See also Claire McGettrick, '"Illegitimate Knowledge": Transitional Justice and Adopted People' (2020), *Éire-Ireland*, 55 (1), pp.181–200.

7 Department of Children, *Final Report of the Commission of Investigation into Mother and Baby Homes*, p.676.

8 *Ibid.*, p.1810.

9 Irene B. Hillary *et al.*, 'Antibody Response in Infants to the Poliomyelitis Component of a Quadruple Vaccine' (1962), *British Medical Journal*, 1 (5285), pp.1098–102.

10 Department of Children, *Final Report of the Commission of Investigation into Mother and Baby Homes*, p.2034. See also Tanya Sillem and Katie Hannon, 'Anatomy of a Scandal', *Prime Time* (RTÉ), October 2011.

11 The infant milk trials were originally reported by the *Irish Examiner* in 2017. See Conall Ó Fátharta, 'New Bessborough Revelations Reveal a Wider Range of Products Tested on Children', *Irish Examiner*, 26 June 2017, https://www.irishexaminer.com/business/arid-20453349.html

12 Lindsey Earner-Byrne, *Mother and Child: Maternity and child welfare in Dublin, 1922–60* (Manchester University Press, 2017), p.192.

13 Paul Michael Garrett, 'The Abnormal Flight: The migration and repatriation of Irish unmarried mothers in Britain' (2000), *Social History*, 25 (3), pp.330–43.

14 Paul Michael Garrett, *Social Work and Irish People in Britain: Historical and contemporary responses to Irish children and families* (The Policy Press, 2004), pp.39–51.

15 Department of Children, *Final Report of the Commission of Investigation into Mother and Baby Homes*, p.387.

16 Garrett, 'The Abnormal Flight', p.340.

17 My thanks to Dr Lorraine Grimes for clarifying this point.

19 Department of Children, *Final Report of the Commission of Investigation into Mother and Baby Homes*, p.1132.

19 *Ibid.*, pp.1132–42.

20 *Ibid.*, p.1054.

21 *Ibid.*, p.1059.

22 *Ibid.*, p.1060.

23 *Ibid.*, p.1062.

24 Catriona Crowe, 'The Commission and the Survivors' (2021), *Dublin Review*, no. 83, https://thedublinreview.com/article/the-commission-and-the-survivors/

25 Hearings were also held in private, despite a number of survivors requesting to testify in public, and those affected did not have access to records collected by the commission about them while testify. The Investigative Committee, on which the findings were based, was not advertised on the commission's website, and many people were unaware of it. In addition, people who requested a hearing at the Investigative Committee were not always granted one. See Maeve O'Rourke, Claire McGettrick, Rod Baker,

Raymond Hill et al., *CLANN: Ireland's Unmarried Mothers and Their Children: Gathering the Data: Principal Submission to the Commission of Investigation into Mother and Baby Homes* (Justice for Magdalenes Research, Adoption Rights Alliance, Hogan Lovells, 2018), pp.129–35.

26 The commission's fifth interim report suggests some of these children may be buried in Cork's Carr's Hill Cemetery but has only been able to confirm this in the case of one child. See Department of Children, Equality, Disability, Integration and Youth, *Commission of Investigation into Mother and Baby Homes and Certain Related Matters, Fifth Interim Report* (2019), https://assets.gov.ie/25783/a141b69a4a3c46fd8daef2010bf51268.pdf, p.36.

27 The commission uncovered very little information about Travellers and the commission did not hear evidence from any survivor who had a disability. Campaign groups such as the Association of Mixed-Race Irish said the evidence had not been examined by an expert with experience of dealing with systemic racism.

28 Section 34 of the 2004 Commissions of Investigation Act states: 'Before submitting the final or an interim report to the specified Minister, a commission shall send a draft of the report, or the relevant part of the draft report, to any person who is identified in or identifiable from the draft report.

29 Conall Ó Fátharta, 'Mother and Baby Home Survivors Demand Vaccine Trial Records', *Irish Examiner*, 23 April 2021, https://www.irishexaminer.com/news/arid-40273322.html

30 Professor Daly said the terms of reference of the Commission of Investigation prohibited including these testimonies, though

legal academics disagree with this interpretation. Minister O'Gorman said the government would be seeking ways to ensure that testimonies given to the Confidential Committee would be 'officially reflected'.

31 Minister O'Gorman wrote to GlaxoSmithKline (GSK) outlining their 'moral and ethical obligation' to people involved in vaccine trials as children. GSK wrote back to say that the company fully co-operated with the commission and would not be paying reparations. GSK said in a letter to the minister published online on 23 March 2021 that the doctors who carried out the trials 'were personally responsible for ensuring they were carried out with the licenses, permits, permissions, and consents required under Irish law and practice at the time'. Professor Irene Hillary and Professor Patrick Meehan, who ran many of the trials, are now deceased.

32 See also: Claire McGettrick. 'Opinion: Our rights as adopted people will not be enshrined in law, they'll be in grave danger', *The Journal*, 21 January 2022, https://www.thejournal.ie/readme/mother-and-baby-5659624=Jan2022

33 Colm Keena, 'Nuns Who Ran the Bessborough Home in Cork Sold Part of the Site for 6.85m', *The Irish Times*, 18 January 2021, https://www.irishtimes.com/news/social-affairs/nuns-who-ran-the-bessborough-home-in-cork-sold-part-of-site-for-6-85m-1.4460685

34 David Dodd and Céile Varley, *Cork Survivors and Supporters Alliance: Submission to the Mother & Baby Homes Commission of Investigation* (2020).